What Are Interactive N

Interactive notebooks are a unique form of note taking. Teachers guide students through creating pages of notes on new topics. Instead of being in the traditional linear, handwritten format, notes are colorful and spread across the pages. Notes also often include drawings, diagrams, and 3-D elements to make the material understandable and relevant. Students are encouraged to complete their notebook pages in ways that make sense to them. With this personalization, no two pages are exactly the same.

Whether you are new to interactive notebooks, or already use interactive notebooks in one or more subject areas, seasonal templates are the perfect addition to any curriculum. New seasons and holidays always hold excitement for students—take advantage of that natural engagement and give students opportunities to practice essential skills in an appealing context. Interactive notebooks make it easy to provide hands-on activities to support, teach, and review during different seasons and holidays throughout the year.

Because of their creative nature, interactive notebooks allow students to be active participants in their own learning. Using seasonally appropriate templates all year long is a fun way to engage students in skill practice and review. For more information on how to integrate seasonal interactive notebooks into your daily and weekly plans, see page 5.

For interactive templates to introduce skills and concepts in math, language arts, word study, and science, pick up the other grade-level books in the Interactive Notebook series.

A student's interactive notebook for roots and affixes

Traditional vs. Seasonal Interactive Notebooks

In many ways, seasonal interactive notebook pages are like traditional interactive notebook pages. However, they are different in several essential ways. Once you understand the similarities and differences between the two types, you can decide how seasonal interactive notebooks will best fit into your schedule and curriculum.

Traditional Interactive Notebooks

- primarily for learning and understanding new skills
- focus on one subject area
- one notebook per subject area
- often created during a whole-group lesson

Both

- fun and engaging
- standards-based
- hands-on learning
- use interactive elements like flaps and pockets
- often include personal connections to content

Seasonal Interactive Notebooks

- primarily for practicing and reviewing skills
- include a variety of subject areas
- may be placed in different notebooks based on subject or stand-alone pages
- can often be created independently

Note about the Autumn Templates

Because autumn is typically the beginning of the school year, the focus of those early weeks is often on reviewing essential skills from the previous grade. So, the interactive templates provided for autumn will include activities that review concepts that are considered below the current grade level. That way, they can be used immediately and will help to ensure students are starting off with last year's concepts solidly in place before you begin to teach new skills and concepts.

How to Use Seasonal Interactive Notebooks

Use the seasonal templates as a time-saving way to incorporate festive fun and excitement in the classroom. This series is a great resource for adding a seasonal element to your math, reading, science, and social studies curriculums. Due to their slightly different nature (see page 4), seasonal templates may work better for your classroom needs by placing them in their own single-subject notebooks, within your existing notebooks, or as stand-alone "lapbooks." Choose the option that works best for your classroom.

Using Traditional Notebooks

Interactive notebooks are usually either single-subject, spiral-bound notebooks, composition books, or three-ring binders with loose-leaf paper. Create a separate seasonal interactive notebook using any of these types. Simply create a table of contents marked with each month and the seasons and holidays that correspond with that month. Place the corresponding templates inside.

Using Existing Interactive Notebooks

Seasonal interactive notebook pages can be used to supplement your students' existing language arts, math, science, or social studies notebooks. Add each template to the subject notebook near the original pages relating to the skill that is being practiced, or add them to the next blank page. For example, if the seasonal notebook page deals with blends and digraphs, have students complete the page in their language arts interactive notebooks.

Using Lapbooks

A lapbook is a file folder that has been folded in a certain manner to accommodate one or more interactive notebook page activities (see diagram below). Lapbooks generally include more information and more hands-on activities relating to a single subject than a typical notebook page. So, students might create a single lapbook about symmetry that includes standard teaching interactive templates as well as the related seasonal template. You may choose to create in-depth subject lapbooks with several different templates and hands-on activities, or create a single seasonal template within a lapbook so it can stand alone.

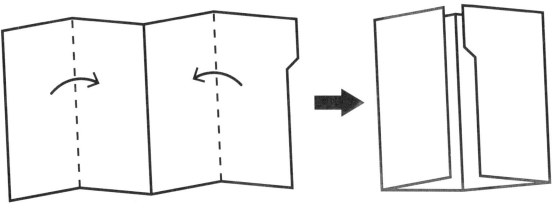

Fold the sides in toward the center.

Managing Seasonal Interactive Notebooks

Make It Independent

- Create a model page for students to refer to. Use it for absent students or place it in a center. Or, place it in a prominent place in the classroom for students to refer to if they don't finish on time.

- As you create the model page, take photos of each step. Use presentation or word document software to show the photos in order, labeled step-by-step (depending on your students' reading levels). Print a copy to keep in the model notebook or post in a center.

Make It Festive

- Instead of copying templates on white paper, use paper in seasonal colors to add a spot of festive color.

- Allow students to use seasonal stickers and other flat decorative objects to complete each page. For example, if students are required to draw a set under a flap, let students place seasonal stickers under the flap instead of drawing. Or, if students are tasked with coming up with a noun, verb, and adjective to describe an object, give them seasonal stickers to place on their pages and have them record the related parts of speech that describe each sticker.

Creating Notebook Pages

- For storing loose pieces, add a pocket to the inside back cover. Use an envelope, a jumbo library pocket, or a resealable plastic bag. Or, tape the bottom and side edges of the two last pages of the notebook together to create a large pocket.

- When writing under flaps, have students trace the outline of each flap so they can visualize the writing boundary.

- Where the dashed line will be hidden on the inside of a fold, have students first fold the piece in the opposite direction so they can see the dashed line. Then, students should fold the piece back the other way along the same fold line to create the fold in the correct direction.

- To avoid losing pieces, have students keep all of their scraps on their desks until they have finished each page.

- To contain paper scraps and avoid multiple trips to the trash can, provide small groups with small buckets or tubs.

- For students who run out of room, keep full and half sheets available. Students can glue these to the bottom of those pages and fold them up when not in use.

Interactive Notebooks

SEASONAL

Grade 4

Credits

Author: Elise Craver
Copy Editor: Christine Schwab

Visit *carsondellosa.com* for correlations to Common Core, state, national, and Canadian provincial standards.

Carson-Dellosa Publishing LLC
PO Box 35665
Greensboro, NC 27425 USA
carsondellosa.com

ISBN 978-1-4838-5028-3
01-305187784

Table of Contents

*These lessons include multiple reproducible pages. They are designed to introduce one or more concepts at a time and can be taught over time. Once assembled, they will use multiple pages in a student's interactive notebook or create more complex pages with more pieces.

Accountability with Interactive Notebooks

As with any other classroom work, students need to be held accountable for their work in interactive notebooks. This will ensure they are doing their best work and that the information included is accurate and will serve as a valuable, error-free resource.

Set Clear Expectations

From the beginning, make sure students know what you expect an interactive notebook page to look like. Use the following questions to outline your expectations.

- What should the edges of the pieces look like after they've been cut out?

- Does it matter if all of the pieces are in the same spot as everyone else's?

- How will the pieces be adhered to the page?

- Can students use pens, colored pencils, markers, etc.?

- What does a neat notebook page look like?

- Should every page have a title? The date?

- How and when should missed pages be completed?

- Where will the notebooks be stored?

- When can students access their notebooks?

- Will students be able to take their notebooks home?

Then, communicate those expectations with one or more of the following:

- Create an anchor chart with students, outlining the expectations.

- Have students glue expectations sheets or rubrics (see pages 8 and 9) to the inside front covers of their notebooks.

- Model, model, model! Create notebook pages along with students so they have a clear vision of what an ideal page looks like.

- Have students sign an interactive notebooks contract to indicate they know the expectations and will follow them.

Have Students Evaluate Themselves

Provide students with copies of the Interactive Notebook Reflection (page 8) so they can assess their own work and reflect on what they did well and what they can improve on. You may then choose to assess the notebook page with the same reflection worksheet and compare the reflections to hold students accountable.

Assess the Notebooks

Don't feel that you have to assess every page. Choose an interval and stick to that. Will you assess every page? Once a week? A month? A quarter? Randomly? It can be time-consuming to do an entire class's worth at once, so do four to six at a time. Use the Grading Rubric (page 9) to clearly and consistently assess students' work.

Name _____   Date _____

Interactive Notebook Reflection

Page Title _____   Page Number _____

I cut neatly.

I colored inside the lines.

I used just the right amount of glue.

I used neat handwriting.

The page is complete and correct.

Color the stars to show the rating you would give your page.

Interactive Notebook Grading Rubric

4

_____	Table of contents is complete.
_____	All notebook pages are included.
_____	All notebook pages are complete.
_____	Notebook pages are neat and organized.
_____	Information is correct.
_____	Pages show personalization, evidence of learning, and original ideas.

3

_____	Table of contents is mostly complete.
_____	One notebook page is missing.
_____	Notebook pages are mostly complete.
_____	Notebook pages are mostly neat and organized.
_____	Information is mostly correct.
_____	Pages show some personalization, evidence of learning, and original ideas.

2

_____	Table of contents is missing a few entries.
_____	A few notebook pages are missing.
_____	A few notebook pages are incomplete.
_____	Notebook pages are somewhat messy and unorganized.
_____	Information has several errors.
_____	Pages show little personalization, evidence of learning, or original ideas.

1

_____	Table of contents is incomplete.
_____	Many notebook pages are missing.
_____	Many notebook pages are incomplete.
_____	Notebook pages are too messy and unorganized to use.
_____	Information is incorrect.
_____	Pages show no personalization, evidence of learning, or original ideas.

Comparing Fall Fractions

Introduction

Review comparing fractions with like numerators and those with like denominators. Emphasize that when the numerators are the same, they should consider the size of the parts. When the denominators are the same, they are comparing how many pieces there are. Display pairs of fractions with the same numerator or same denominator. Have students use their hands to make greater than, less than, or equal signs to compare each set.

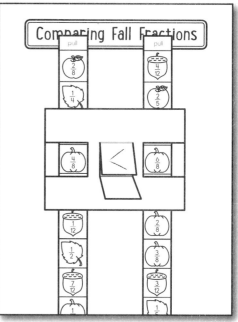

Creating the Notebook Page

Guide students through the following steps to complete the right-hand page in their notebooks.

1. Add a Table of Contents entry for the Comparing Fall Fractions pages.

2. Cut out the title and glue it to the top of the page.

3. Cut out the large rectangle. Cut on the solid lines to create a flap in the center of each side. Apply glue to the back of the center section and the center flaps on each side and attach it to the page. The top and bottom flaps on each side should not be attached to the page.

4. Cut out the piece with the equal sign. Apply glue to the gray glue section on the large rectangle and attach the center section of the equal sign so the flaps open up and down.

5. Flip down the top flap and draw a less than symbol (<) on it. Flip up the bottom flap and draw a greater than symbol (>) on it.

6. Cut out the fraction strips. Apply glue to the gray glue sections and place the other strips on top to create two long fraction strips with *pull* on the top and bottom of each strip.

7. Slide each fraction strip between the flaps on the large rectangle so a single fraction shows in each space to the left and right of the <, =, > piece. If desired, apply glue to the backs of the flaps and attach them to the page to secure each strip in place. The strip should slide freely.

8. Slide the strips to show two fractions with the same art (for example, leaf and leaf). Unfold the flaps in the center to create a true fraction comparison. If students are ready to compare fractions with different numerators and denominators, they may compare any two fractions, regardless of art. Fold the strips before closing the notebook.

Reflect on Learning

To complete the left-hand page, have students answer the following question: *If you had to share some of your holiday candy with someone, would you rather give them 1/3 or 1/4 of your candy? Why?*

© Carson-Dellosa • CD-105017

Comparing Fall Fractions

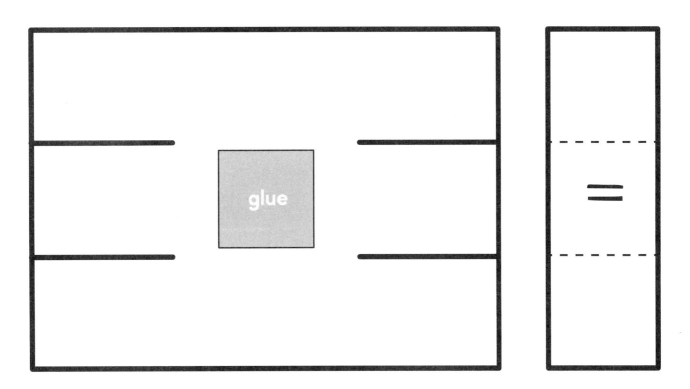

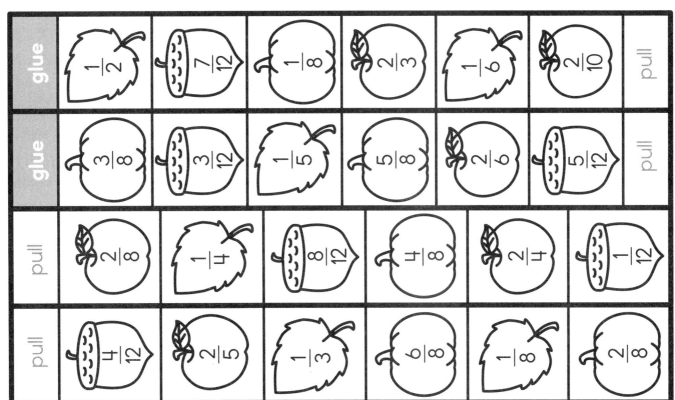

Columbus Day Persuasive Writing

Introduction

As a class, create a bubble map showing everything students know about Christopher Columbus. Allow students to share their information and add it to the bubble map. Use this time to correct any misconceptions.

Creating the Notebook Page

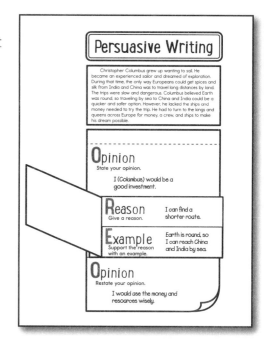

Guide students through the following steps to complete the right-hand page in their notebooks.

1. Add a Table of Contents entry for the Columbus Day Persuasive Writing pages.

2. Cut out the title and glue it to the top of the page.

3. Cut out the passage and glue it below the title.

4. Cut out the large *Opinion* flap. Apply glue to the back of the top section and attach it to the page below the passage.

5. Cut out the two *Reason/Example* flaps. Apply glue to the gray glue section on one and stack the other on top. Then, apply glue to the gray glue section on the large *Opinion* flap and attach the small double flap to it.

6. Read the passage. Then, discuss how effective persuasive writing establishes an opinion and backs that opinion up with several reasons. Including a related example makes each reason stronger. Then, it should conclude by restating the opinion.

7. Pretend you are Columbus and need to write a letter to the queen asking for money and resources for exploration. Using the information from the passage, as well as any other related sources, complete the graphic organizer. Then, use the graphic organizer to write a draft of your letter under the flap.

8. If desired, you may use this graphic organizer with other persuasive writing prompts. Simply discard the title and passage.

Reflect on Learning

To complete the left-hand page, have students make a copy of the graphic organizer and complete it from the queen's point of view. If time allows, let them write a letter back from the queen to Columbus, using their new graphic organizers as the basis.

Persuasive Writing

Christopher Columbus grew up wanting to sail. He became an experienced sailor and dreamed of exploration. During that time, the only way Europeans could get spices and silk from India and China was to travel long distances by land. The trips were slow and dangerous. Columbus believed Earth was round, so traveling by sea to China and India could be a quicker and safer option. However, he lacked the ships and money needed to try the trip. He had to turn to the kings and queens across Europe for money, a crew, and ships to make his dream possible.

Opinion
State your opinion.

Reason
Give a reason.

Example
Support the reason with an example.

Opinion
Restate your opinion.

Reason
Give a reason.

Example
Support the reason with an example.

Reason
Give a reason.

Example
Support the reason with an example.

glue

Candy Corn Area and Perimeter

Introduction

Review the difference between area and perimeter. Give each student an index card. Discuss how the perimeter is the measure of the distance around the outside of a shape. Have students write *perimeter* repeatedly around the outer edges of the index card. Discuss how area is the measure of the space inside a shape or the 2-D space a shape takes up. Have students write *AREA* large enough to fill the interior of the index card. Have students glue these "cheat sheets" to the left-hand page opposite this activity in their notebooks.

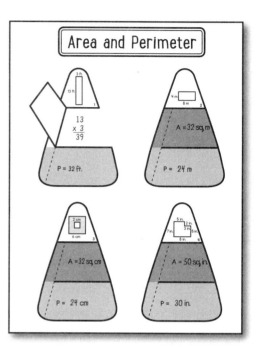

Creating the Notebook Page

Guide students through the following steps to complete the right-hand page in their notebooks.

1. Add a Table of Contents entry for the Candy Corn Area and Perimeter pages.

2. Cut out the title and glue it to the top of the page.

3. Cut out each candy corn. Each one is made of two pieces: the top section showing the shape, and the two-flap flap book. Glue each top section to the page, leaving space below each for the flap book. Cut on the solid lines to create two flaps on each flap book. Then, apply glue to the backs of the left sections on the flap books and attach each one below a top section to create four candy corns on the page.

4. For each candy corn, find the area and perimeter of the shape given. Write the answers on each flap. Under the flap, draw or write how you found the area or perimeter.

Reflect on Learning

To complete the left-hand page, challenge students to draw a shape that has an area of 16 square centimeters and a perimeter of 20 centimeters.

Answer Key
1. A = 39 sq. ft.; P = 32 ft.; 2. A = 32 sq. m; P = 24 m; 3. A = 32 sq. cm; P = 24 cm; 4. A = 50 sq. in.; P = 30 in.; Reflect: One possible solution is a rectangle 2 centimeters wide and 8 centimeters long.

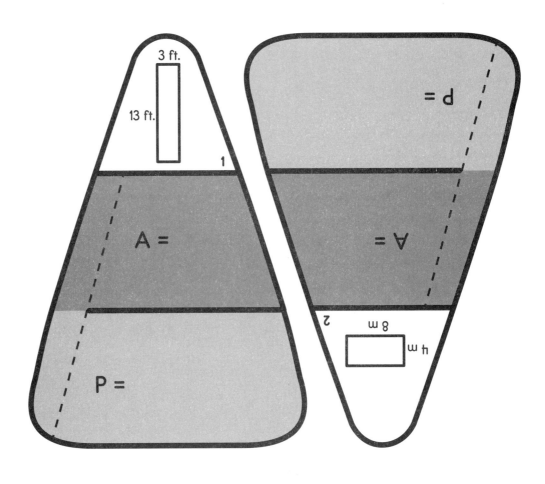

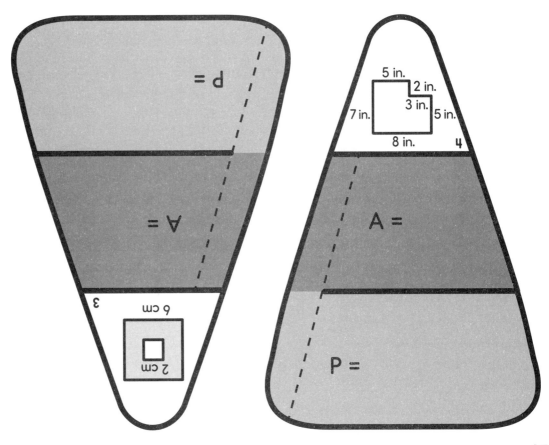

Spider Myth Reading Comprehension

You may choose to study the myth with only the close reading activity (page 18), only the story elements activities (page 19), or both. The templates can easily be used with any other literature piece.

Introduction

Review myths, fables, and legends. Write characteristics of each story type on sentence strips. Write *Myth*, *Fable*, and *Legend* on the board. Have the class place each characteristic under the correct header. Discuss each story type.

Creating the Notebook Page

Guide students through the following steps to complete the right-hand page in their notebooks.

1. Add a Table of Contents entry for the Spider Myth Reading Comprehension pages.

2. Cut out the title and glue it to the top of the page.

3. Cut out the passage (page 17) and glue it to the left-hand page. If desired, glue down only the top so it functions as a flap and the activities can be placed under the flap.

(Not all pieces are shown.)

4. Cut out the flaps on page 18. Apply glue to the backs of the left sections and attach one or all to a new page.

5. Read the story each of three times. On each flap, mark how you read it, choose an area to focus on, and record your observations related to that focus. Use a different color to mark the text each time and shade the left-hand section the same color for clarity. Under each flap, write one to two sentences about the chosen focus area. For example, if *theme* was chosen, define the theme and give a supporting example.

6. Cut out the story element pieces (page 19). Apply glue to the backs of the narrow sections of the *Setting* and *Problem* flap books, the *THEME* flap, and the *Point of View* pocket and attach them to the page. Choose the matching point of view piece, glue it to the *pull* piece, and discard the others. Slide it in the *Point of View* pocket. Fold back and forth on the dashed lines of the *Plot* piece to create an accordion fold. Apply glue to the back of the last section and attach it to the page. Glue the *Genre* piece to the page. Record the story elements of "The Myth of Arachne" by writing the requested information on or under each piece.

Reflect on Learning

To complete the left-hand page, have students explain the purpose of the myth of Arachne and state its moral or theme.

The Myth of Arachne

Long ago, in a small Greek town, there lived a young woman named Arachne. She was known far and wide as an accomplished spinner. She spun yarn on her spindle every morning and wove the most beautiful cloths on her loom every evening. People came from miles around to see her weavings of flax, wool, and silk. Everyone said they seemed to be woven of clouds and threads of gold.

Arachne was happy as she sat in the shade, weaving. "There is no other yarn as fine as mine," she boasted, "nor is there any other cloth as beautiful and rare." When people asked her who had taught her, she claimed she had taught herself.

When someone suggested that the goddess Athena might have taught her, Arachne replied, "That is not possible! What could she teach me? Can she spin yarn such as mine or weave such beautiful cloths of clouds and gold, sunlight and stars? What could she possibly teach me, the best weaver in the world?"

Just then, a tall woman with sharp, bright eyes said, "I am Athena, the goddess of arts and crafts and wisdom. I heard what you said. Are you sure you are better than me?" Arachne squirmed in her seat but answered, "Yes."

"Let's hold a contest to find out if that is true," Athena replied. "We will both weave cloths to be judged by the great Zeus. If your cloth is more beautiful than mine, I will never weave again. But, if my cloth is better than yours, you will never again use a loom or spindle." Arachne agreed.

Three days later, hordes of people arrived for the contest. The great Zeus sat on his throne in the clouds to watch. Arachne began to weave with her finest silk. She wove a web of light and shadow, so fine that it could float on air yet so strong it could trap a wild beast. The magnificent colors glimmered in the sun. Surely, she was the best weaver.

Then, Athena began to weave. She gathered sunlight, moonlight, and the sweetness of the clouds. She used the jewel tones of the sky, the yellows and greens of summer, and the oranges and purples of autumn. She wove a cloth that sang of the world and its blossoms, jewels, mountains, and creatures. All who saw it gasped, then smiled in delight and wonder.

"Oh!" cried Arachne. "It's beautiful! I'm so ashamed." She began to cry. "I cannot live if I can't spin and weave. It is my life!" Athena looked at the sobbing girl and pitied her.

"Stop crying," Athena said. "You can never touch a loom or spindle again. But, I know you will never be happy if you cannot weave." And with that, Athena turned Arachne into a spider. She ran off and immediately began to spin and weave a web. She was happy again.

	I read	**Focus**	**What I Noticed**
1st Read	☐ alone. ☐ with a partner. ☐ with a group. ☐ with the teacher.	theme key details story elements summary	• _____ • _____ • _____ • _____ • _____ • _____
2nd Read	☐ alone. ☐ with a partner. ☐ with a group. ☐ with the teacher.	word choice overall structure narrator's or main character's point of view	• _____ • _____ • _____ • _____ • _____ • _____
3rd Read	☐ alone. ☐ with a partner. ☐ with a group. ☐ with the teacher.	making an inference my opinion or connection comparison to similar texts	• _____ • _____ • _____ • _____ • _____ • _____

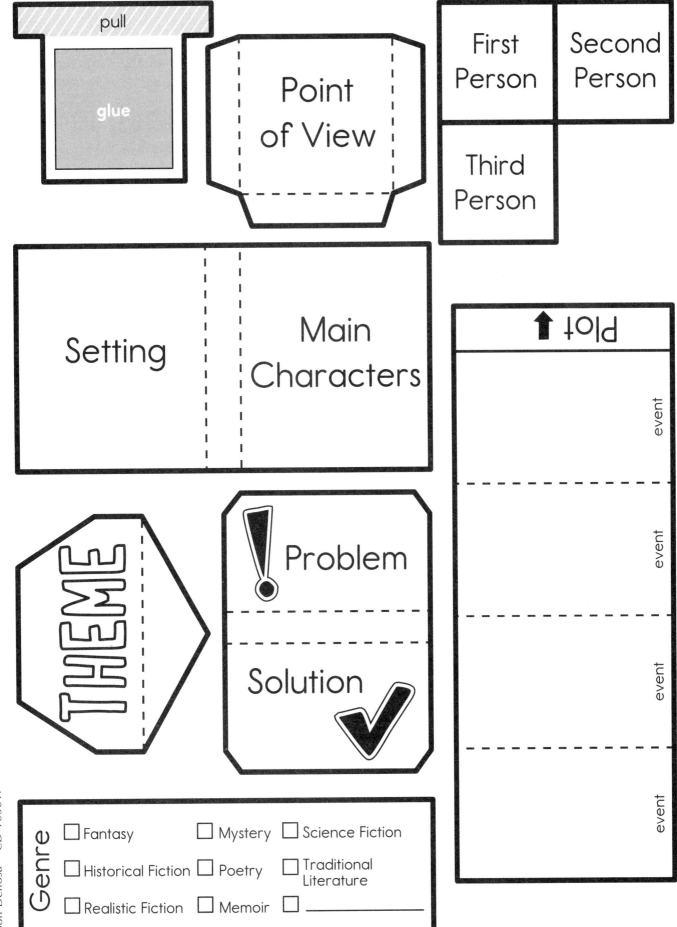

pull

glue

Point
of View

First
Person

Second
Person

Third
Person

Setting

Main
Characters

Plot ↑

event

event

event

event

THEME

Problem

Solution

Genre

☐ Fantasy   ☐ Mystery   ☐ Science Fiction

☐ Historical Fiction   ☐ Poetry   ☐ Traditional
                                          Literature

☐ Realistic Fiction   ☐ Memoir   ☐ _____

Government and Elections

Introduction

Challenge students to brainstorm as many election vocabulary words as they can. Record a list on the board. Briefly define each word orally to ensure all students understand the vocabulary.

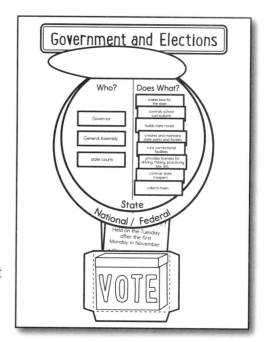

Creating the Notebook Page

Guide students through the following steps to complete the right-hand page in their notebooks.

1. Add a Table of Contents entry for the Government and Elections pages.

2. Cut out the title and glue it to the top of the page.

3. Cut out the three circle flaps (pages 21–22). Apply glue to the gray glue sections and stack the flaps from largest to smallest to create a stacked three-flap flap book. Apply glue to the back of the top section of the stacked flap book and attach it to the page.

4. Cut out the *makes laws for* set of pieces (page 21). Decide which level of government each statement applies to and glue it on the correct flap, under the matching question. Repeat with each set of pieces (pages 21–23). Cut out only one set of pieces at a time to avoid losing pieces and to focus on one area of people or duties at a time.

5. Cut out the *VOTE* pocket. Apply glue to the backs of the three flaps and attach it to the page.

6. Cut out the *Presidential, Local,* and *Midterm Elections* pieces. Apply glue to the backs of the *Local* and *Midterm* pieces and fold on the dashed lines to create double-sided "ballots."

7. Complete each "ballot." On the *Midterm* piece, write the names of your state's senators and your district's representative(s) under the matching bullets. Store them in the *VOTE* pocket.

Reflect on Learning

To complete the left-hand page, have students complete a triple Venn diagram to compare and contrast the three levels of government.

Answer Key
National—Who: President; Congress; Supreme Court; Does What: makes laws for the country; controls the military; works with other countries; prints money; runs the post office; creates and maintains national parks; helps pay for construction and maintenance of major roads; collects taxes; **State**—Who: Governor; General Assembly; state courts; Does What: makes laws for the state; controls school curriculums; builds state roads; creates and maintains parks and forests; runs correctional facilities; provides licenses for driving, fishing, practicing law, etc.; controls state troopers; collects taxes; **Local**—Who: Mayor; local courts; City Council and Commissioners; Does What: solves community problems; repairs roads; provides schools and teachers; provides libraries, parks, and sports facilities; provides emergency services and community police; controls electricity, natural gas, and water; collects garbage; collects property taxes

Government and Elections

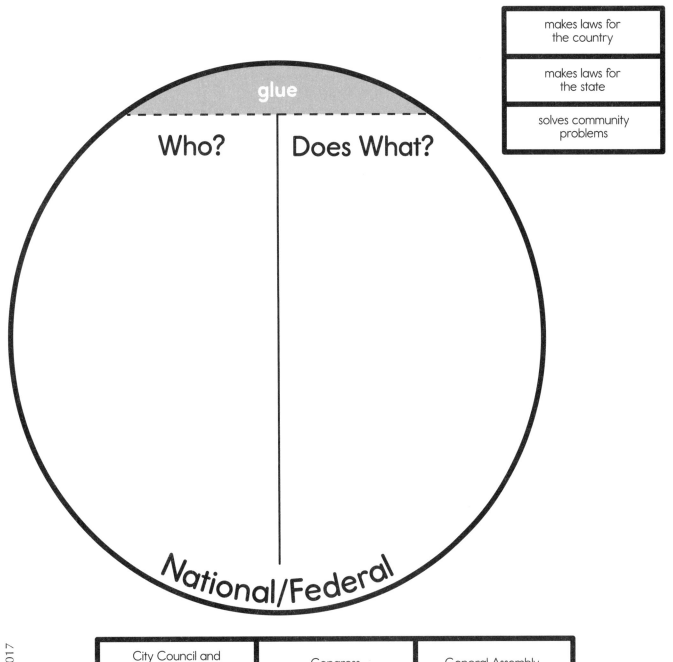

makes laws for the country	
makes laws for the state	
solves community problems	

Who? | Does What?

National/Federal

City Council and Commissioners	Congress	General Assembly
Governor	local courts	Mayor
President	state courts	Supreme Court

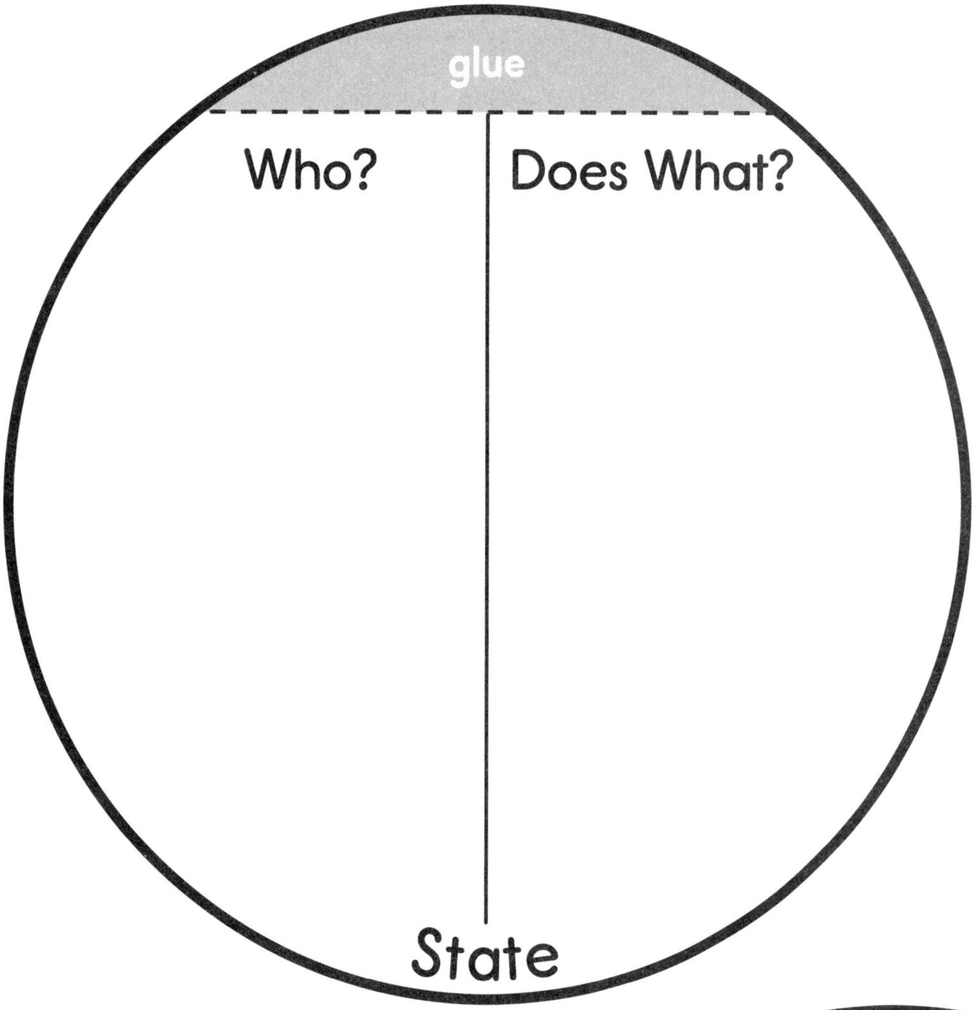

State (circle)

glue

Who? | **Does What?**

State

State answer strips (right box)

- helps pay for construction and maintenance of major roads
- builds state roads
- repairs roads
- creates and maintains national parks
- creates and maintains state parks and forests
- provides libraries, parks, and sports facilities
- controls the military
- controls state troopers
- provides emergency services and community police

Local answer strips (left box)

- works with other countries
- runs the post office
- runs correctional facilities
- controls school curriculums
- provides licenses for driving, fishing, practicing law, etc.
- provides schools and teachers
- controls electricity, natural gas, and water
- collects garbage

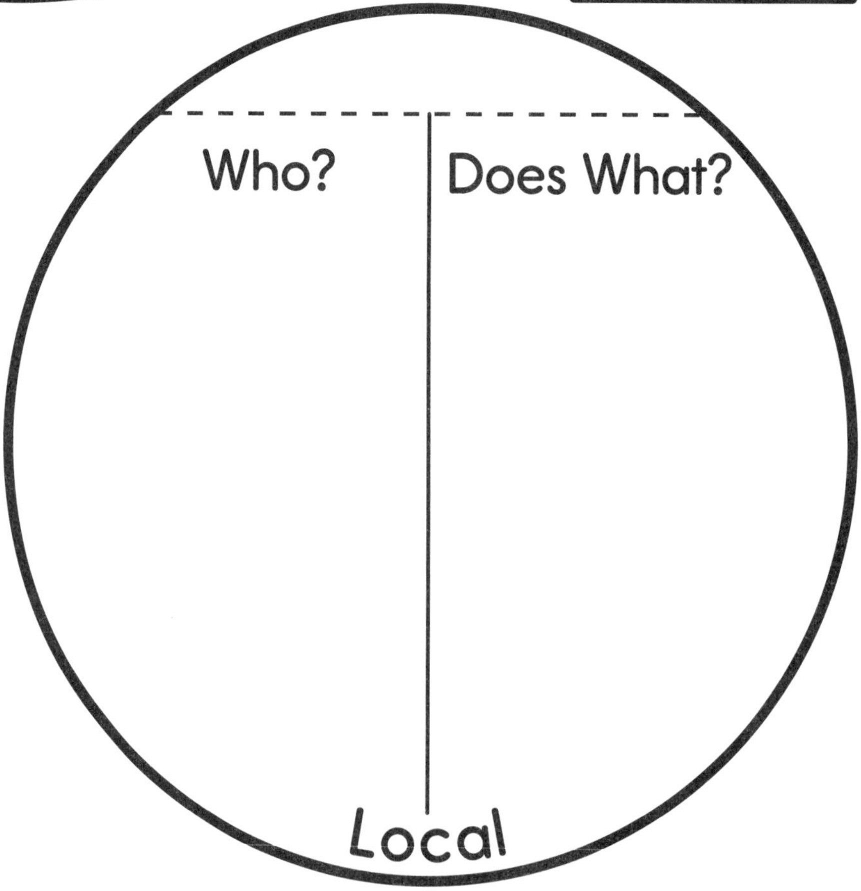

Local (circle)

Who? | **Does What?**

Local

prints money	collects taxes	collects taxes	collects property taxes

(For use with pages 21 and 22.)

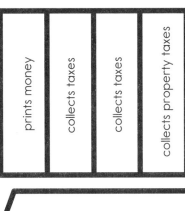

Midterm Elections

_____ (my state)

- _____ Senate seats
- _____ House seats
- The next midterm election is _____ .

S	M	T	W	TH	F	S
			1	2	3	4
5	6	★	8	9	10	11
12	13	14	15	16	17	18

Held on the Tuesday after the first Monday in November

- Occur every _____ years

Citizens vote for
- all _____ House of Representatives seats.
- about _____ of the Senate seats.

Presidential Election

S	M	T	W	TH	F	S
			1	2	3	4
5	6	★	8	9	10	11
12	13	14	15	16	17	18

Held on the Tuesday after the first Monday in November

- Occurs every _____ years
- The next presidential election is _____
  _____ .

Local Elections

- Occur

Voting for other local offices, including
- ☐ attorneys
- ☐ treasurer
- ☐ comptrollers
- ☐ auditors
- ☐ judges
- ☐ court clerks
- ☐ police chief or sheriff
- ☐ school board members and president
- ☐ councilmen/aldermen
- ☐ _____
- ☐ _____
- ☐ _____

- Elected Officials

Thanksgiving Paired Passages

Because the firsthand account passage is from the 1800s, it includes some difficult language. The Introduction activity is intended to pre-teach and reinforce the new vocabulary.

Introduction

Before the lesson, write each of the following words on a card, along with a simple definition for each: *provision, sufficient, multitude, abundance, prosperity, precedence, savory, niche, tribute,* and *gratitude.* Divide students into 10 groups and give each group a vocabulary word. Groups should come up with a related motion for their word. For example, for *savory,* students might mime eating a bite of food and rubbing their bellies. As groups share their words, definitions, and motions, the rest of the class should repeat the motions. Encourage students to use the motions throughout the activity to help remember the definitions.

Thanksgiving Past and Present

The table . . . was now intended for the whole household, every child having a seat on this occasion; and the more the better, it being considered an honor for a man to sit down to his Thanksgiving dinner surrounded by a large family. The provision is always sufficient for a multitude, every family in the country being, at this season of the year, plentifully supplied, and every one proud of displaying his abundance and prosperity. The roasted turkey took precedence on this occasion, being placed at the head of the table; and well did it become its lordly station, sending forth the rich odor of its savory stuffing, and finely covered with the froth of the basting . . .

There was a huge plum pudding, custards and pies of every name and description ever known in Yankee land; yet the pumpkin pie occupied the most distinguished niche . . .

[It] is considered as an appropriate tribute of gratitude . . . to set apart one day of Thanksgiving in each year; and autumn is the time when the overflowing garners of America call for the expression of joyful gratitude.

Excerpted from *Northwood* by Sarah Josepha Hale

While we often hear about the first Thanksgiving in the Plymouth Colony in 1621, the first modern Thanksgiving feast didn't occur until 200 years later. A letter written by Edward Winslow in 1621 about the Plymouth Thanksgiving was rediscovered in the 1800s. It was clear that the celebration was intended to be a single event to give thanks for the good harvest, instead of a yearly celebration. A Boston publisher printed the short letter and named it the "First Thanksgiving." After that, several states made it a state holiday, and magazine editor Sarah Josepha Hale continued to suggest that it become a national holiday. In 1863, President Lincoln officially made Thanksgiving Day a national holiday.

Thanksgiving celebrations in the 1800s included many foods we continue to eat today, including turkey, pumpkin pie, potatoes, cranberry relish, and biscuits. It also included less familiar foods like oyster soup and mince pies. While turkey wasn't the focus of the 1621 Thanksgiving, it became the main dish in the 1800s. They were cooked over a hearth. The heart of the holiday was spending time with family and friends as well as prayer and worship. Common after-dinner activities often included shooting matches, singing, and . . .

This is a firsthand account.

It uses "we." The author was not at the event.

primary source	first person point of view		secondary source	third person point of view
includes personal opinions	includes emotions		gives key facts	includes facts from different sources
includes specific details	written by someone who was there		based on research	author was not at the event
	diaries/journals			description of events

Creating the Notebook Page

Guide students through the following steps to complete the right-hand page in their notebooks.

1. Add a Table of Contents entry for the Thanksgiving Paired Passages pages.

2. Cut out the title and glue it to the top of the page.

3. Cut out the two passage flaps. Apply glue to the backs of the top sections and attach them to the page.

4. Read each passage.

5. Cut out the *firsthand* and *secondhand account* pieces. Glue each piece to the bottom of the matching passage. Under each flap, explain why the passage is a firsthand or secondhand account.

6. Cut out the characteristic pieces. Glue each piece below the matching type of passage. It may be helpful to draw a line to separate the sections.

Reflect on Learning

To complete the left-hand page, have students explain why it is important to read and compare both firsthand and secondhand accounts of the same event.

Answer Key
Firsthand accounts: primary source, first person point of view, includes personal opinions, includes emotions, includes specific details, written by someone who was there, diaries/journals; Secondhand accounts: secondary source, third person point of view, gives key facts, includes facts from different sources, based on research, description of events, author was not at the event

The table . . . was now intended for the whole household, every child having a seat on this occasion; and the more the better, it being considered an honor for a man to sit down to his Thanksgiving dinner surrounded by a large family. The provision is always sufficient for a multitude, every farmer in the country being, at this season of the year, plentifully supplied, and every one proud of displaying his abundance and prosperity. The roasted turkey took precedence on this occasion, being placed at the head of the table; and well did it become its lordly station, sending forth the rich odor of its savory stuffing, and finely covered with the froth of the basting . . . .

There was a huge plum pudding, custards and pies of every name and description ever known in Yankee land; yet the pumpkin pie occupied the most distinguished niche . . . .

[It] is considered as an appropriate tribute of gratitude . . . to set apart one day of Thanksgiving in each year; and autumn is the time when the overflowing garners of America call for this expression of joyful gratitude.

Excerpted from *Northwood* by Sarah Josepha Hale

This is a

While we often hear about the first Thanksgiving in the Plymouth Colony in 1621, the first modern Thanksgiving feast didn't occur until 200 years later. A letter written by Edward Winslow in 1621 about the Plymouth Thanksgiving was rediscovered in the 1800s. It was clear that the celebration was intended to be a single event to give thanks for the good harvest, instead of a yearly celebration. A Boston publisher printed the short letter and named the meal the "First Thanksgiving." After that, several states made it a state holiday, and magazine editor Sarah Josepha Hale continued to suggest that it become a national holiday. In 1863, President Lincoln officially made Thanksgiving Day a national holiday.

Thanksgiving celebrations in the 1800s included many foods we continue to eat today, including turkey, pumpkin pie, potatoes, cranberry relish, and biscuits. They also included less familiar foods like oyster soup and mince pies. While turkey wasn't the focus of the 1621 Thanksgiving, it became the main dish in the 1800s. They were cooked over a hearth. The heart of the holiday was spending time with family and friends as well as in prayer and worship. Common after-dinner activities often included shooting matches, singing, and storytelling. Nineteenth century Thanksgivings were the start of many of the holiday traditions we recognize today.

This is a

Thanksgiving Past and Present

author was not at the event	based on research
description of events	diaries/journals
first person point of view	gives key facts
includes emotions	includes facts from different sources
includes personal opinions	includes specific details
primary source	secondary source
third person point of view	written by someone who was there

secondhand account.

firsthand account.

Thanksgiving Punctuating Dialogue

Introduction

Before the lesson, write alternative words for *said* on sentence strips. Have each student choose one. Write a statement on the board, such as *I can't believe this is happening*, and have students read it with their tag line. They should place their tag lines at the end of the quote. With the first tag line used, review punctuating dialogue as you add the correct punctuation marks. Discuss tag lines and have other students try their tag lines at the beginning or middle of the quote and change the punctuation to match. Discuss how tag lines can change the feeling of a statement.

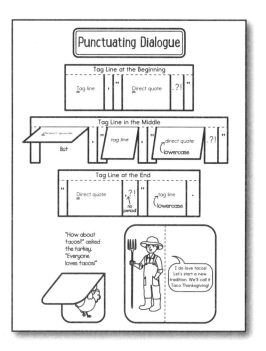

Creating the Notebook Page

Guide students through the following steps to complete the right-hand page in their notebooks.

1. Add a Table of Contents entry for the Thanksgiving Punctuating Dialogue pages.

2. Cut out the title and glue it to the top of the page.

3. Cut out the three *Tag Line* flap books. Cut on the solid lines to create flaps. Apply glue to the backs of the top sections and attach them to the page (from top to bottom: *Beginning, Middle, End*).

4. On top of each flap, write any extra notes, such as example tag lines, where capital letters occur, or the name of each punctuation mark. Discuss how the ending punctuation changes from a period to a comma in certain cases.

5. Cut out the three quote pieces. Match each one to the correct *Tag Line* flap book based on the location of the tag line in the quote. Then, rewrite each quote under the matching flaps. It may be helpful to circle or highlight important information, such as the locations of capital letters or the ending punctuation used. Discard the quote pieces.

6. Cut out the farmer and turkey flaps. Apply glue to the backs of the turkey and farmer sections and attach them to the bottom of the page.

7. Finish the conversation from the tag line quote pieces under the flaps. What did the turkey say next? Then, what did the farmer say? Under each flap, rewrite the quote with the tag line in a spot of your choosing. Use correct punctuation.

Reflect on Learning

To complete the left-hand page, have students write a full conversation where the turkey tries to convince the farmer not to eat him for Thanksgiving dinner.

Punctuating Dialogue

Tag Line at the Beginning

| Tag line | , | " | Direct quote | .?! | " |

Tag Line at the End

| " | Direct quote | ,?! | " | tag line | . |

Tag Line in the Middle

| " | Direct quote | , | " | tag line | , | " | direct quote | .?! | " |

Farmer Brown stated,
"Turkey is traditional."

"But," argued the turkey,
"pizza tastes better!"

"Yes, but we eat it too often,"
Farmer Brown replied.

How about tacos? Everyone loves tacos!

I do love tacos! Let's start a new tradition. We'll call it Taco Thanksgiving!

Native American Tribes

Introduction

Ask students to share what they think about when they hear the terms *Native American* or *American Indian*. Students may share things like horses, feathered headdresses, tepees, arrowheads, etc. Discuss how these characteristics may be true of some tribes, but that not all tribes used horses, lived in tepees, etc. Each tribe has its own cultural identity and unique differences. Emphasize that while many characteristics are generally true for large regions, students should be sensitive to tribal differences.

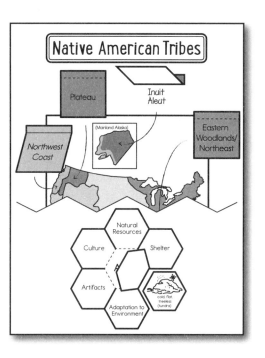

Creating the Notebook Page

Guide students through the following steps to complete the right-hand page in their notebooks.

1. Add a Table of Contents entry for the Native American Tribes pages.

2. Cut out the title and glue it to the top of the page.

3. Cut out the map and glue it to the center of the page.

4. Cut out the region flaps. Identify each region on the map and color it and the flap the same color. Apply glue to the backs of the top sections of the flaps and glue them near the region on the map.

5. Under each flap, record the names of some specific tribes from that region. Identify the region near your home and any tribes local to that area. Add a star to the map to identify your rough location.

6. Cut out a hexagon flap book (pages 30–33). Cut on the solid lines to create six flaps. Apply glue to the back of the center section and attach it to the page. Use a new notebook page for each flap book.

7. Cut out the hexagon pieces. Glue them under the matching flaps. Discuss the broad characteristics common to many tribes in the area. Note that these characteristics may not apply to each tribe within the region. If desired, add more information to the back of each flap or in the space around the flap book, including information about transportation, specific foods eaten, names of local tribes, etc.

Reflect on Learning

To complete the left-hand page, choose two tribal regions and compare and contrast their characteristics.

Native American Tribes

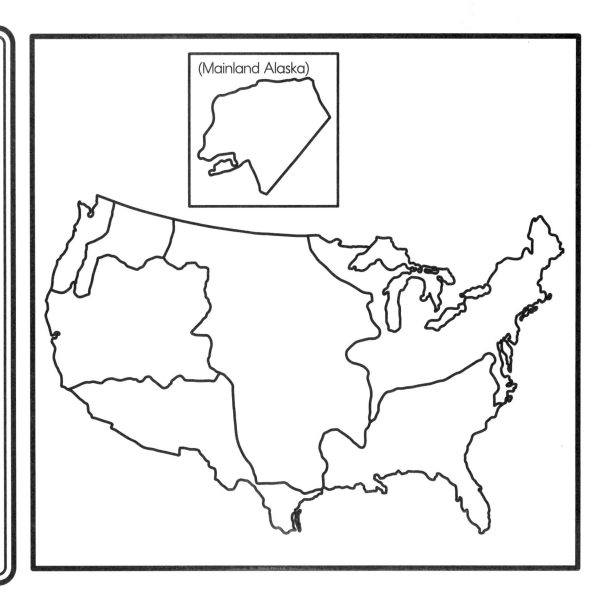

(Mainland Alaska)

Arctic	Northwest Coast	Plateau	Great Basin
Southwest	Plains	Eastern Woodlands/ Northeast	Southeast

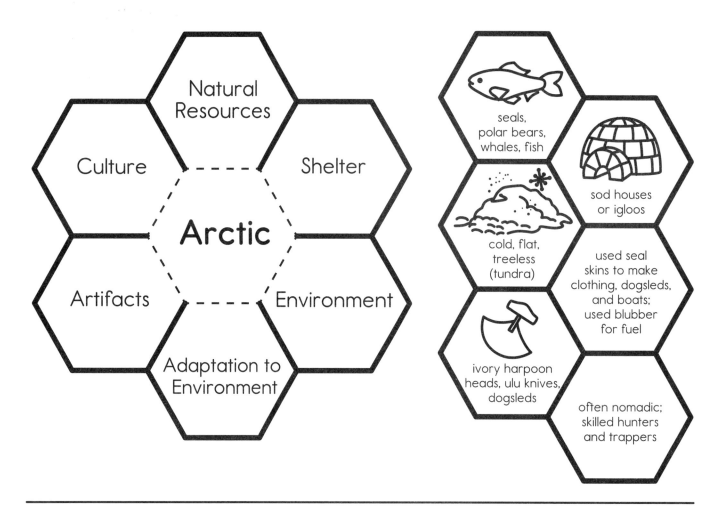

Arctic

- Natural Resources
- Shelter
- Culture
- Artifacts
- Environment
- Adaptation to Environment

- seals, polar bears, whales, fish
- sod houses or igloos
- cold, flat, treeless (tundra)
- used seal skins to make clothing, dogsleds, and boats; used blubber for fuel
- ivory harpoon heads, ulu knives, dogsleds
- often nomadic; skilled hunters and trappers

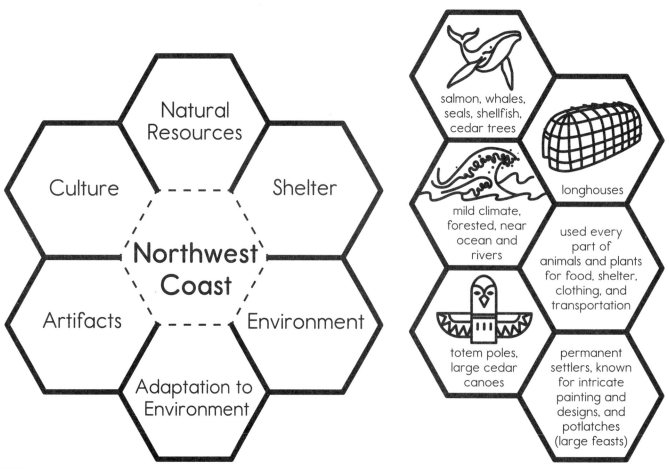

Northwest Coast

- Natural Resources
- Shelter
- Culture
- Artifacts
- Environment
- Adaptation to Environment

- salmon, whales, seals, shellfish, cedar trees
- longhouses
- mild climate, forested, near ocean and rivers
- used every part of animals and plants for food, shelter, clothing, and transportation
- totem poles, large cedar canoes
- permanent settlers, known for intricate painting and designs, and potlatches (large feasts)

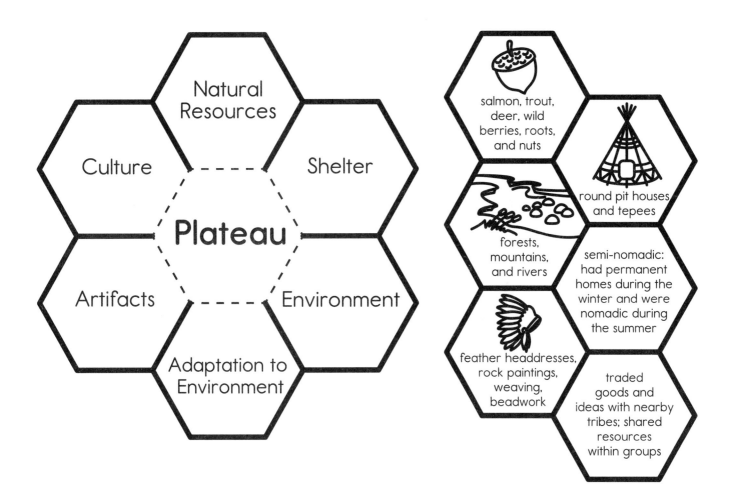

Plateau

- Natural Resources
- Culture
- Shelter
- Artifacts
- Environment
- Adaptation to Environment

salmon, trout, deer, wild berries, roots, and nuts

round pit houses and tepees

forests, mountains, and rivers

semi-nomadic: had permanent homes during the winter and were nomadic during the summer

feather headdresses, rock paintings, weaving, beadwork

traded goods and ideas with nearby tribes; shared resources within groups

Great Basin

- Natural Resources
- Culture
- Shelter
- Artifacts
- Environment
- Adaptation to Environment

roots, seeds, nuts, wild rice, birds, and small animals

lean-tos and wikiups made of saplings, grass, and brush

dry, with deserts and salt flats

nomadic to forage for food, so shelter was easy to build and move

stone tools, woven baskets

nomadic hunter-gatherers

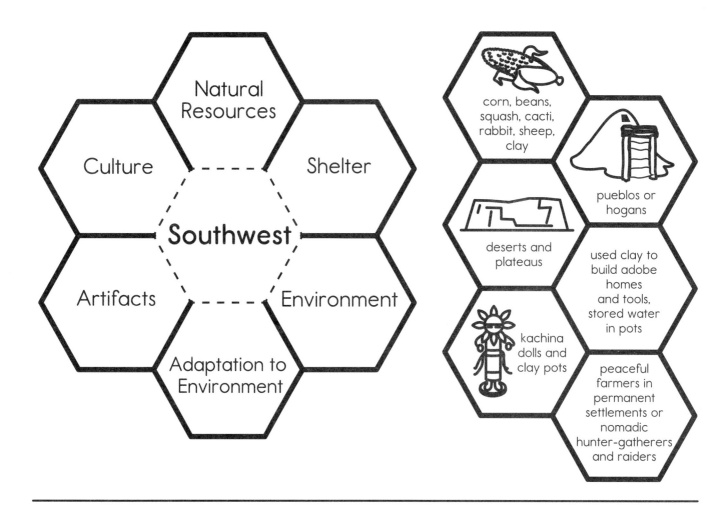

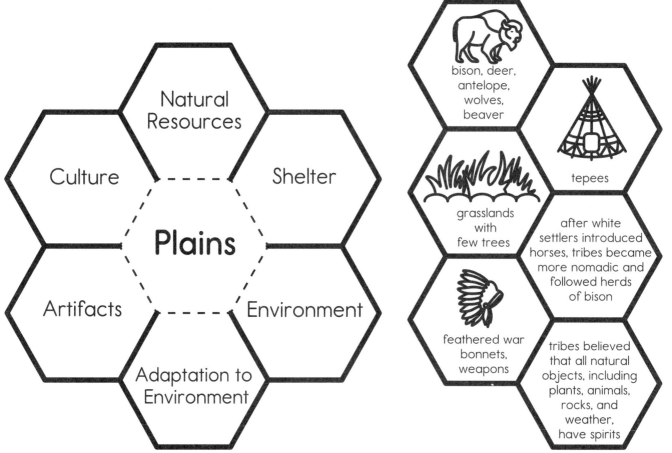

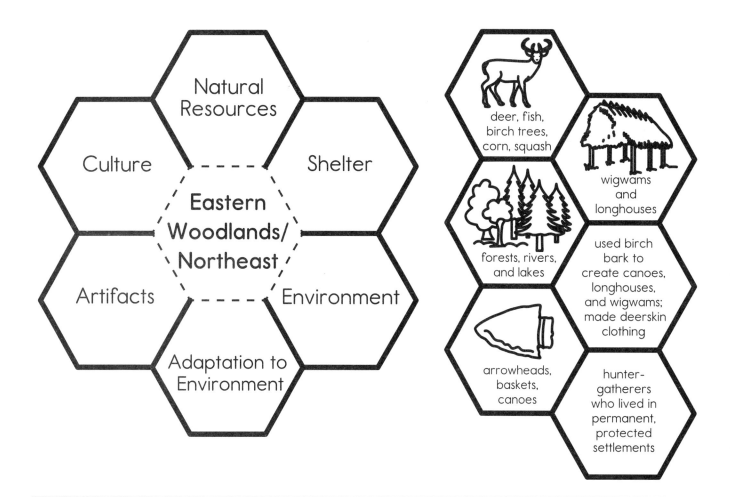

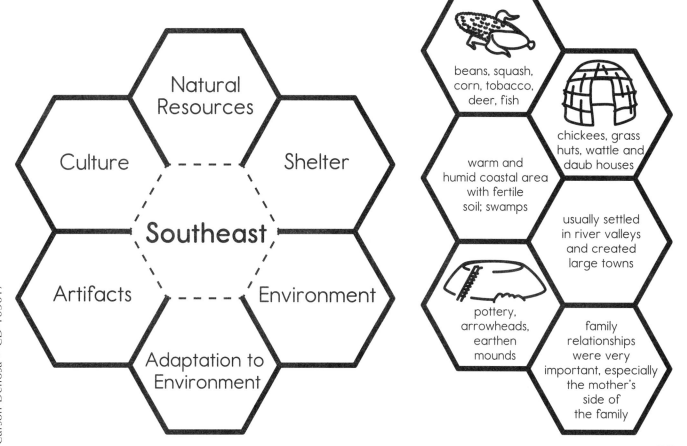

Pumpkin Pie Decomposing Fractions

Introduction

Before the lesson, gather two colors of square sticky notes. Give each student one sticky note in one color or the other. Call groups of students to the board to create rectangles with their collective sticky notes. For each rectangle created, discuss the total number of parts, what fraction of the shape is one color versus the other, and the fraction of a single sticky note. Emphasize each time that a single sticky note is one out of the whole and show the related unit fraction.

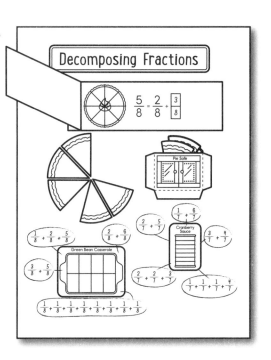

Creating the Notebook Page

Guide students through the following steps to complete the right-hand page in their notebooks.

1. Add a Table of Contents entry for the Pumpkin Pie Decomposing Fractions pages.

2. Cut out the title and glue it to the top of the page.

3. Cut out the three flaps. Apply glue to the gray glue sections and stack the flaps to create a stacked three-flap flap book. Apply glue to the back of the left section and attach it to the page below the title.

4. Cut out the *Pie Safe* pocket. Apply glue to the backs of the three flaps and attach it to the page below the flap book.

5. Cut out the pumpkin pie piece and cut on the solid lines to create eight slices. When not in use, store the pieces in the *Pie Safe* pocket.

6. Use the pie pieces to model and complete each flap in the flap book. Under the last flap, record your own unique decomposition for the fraction 5/8.

7. Cut out the *Green Bean Casserole* and *Cranberry Sauce* pieces. Glue them to the bottom of the page, leaving space around each one. Make a bubble map around each showing different possible decompositions.

Reflect on Learning

To complete the left-hand page, have students choose several decompositions from the right-hand page and show each one as a number bond. Then, students should explain how number bonds and decomposing fractions are related to adding and subtracting fractions with like denominators.

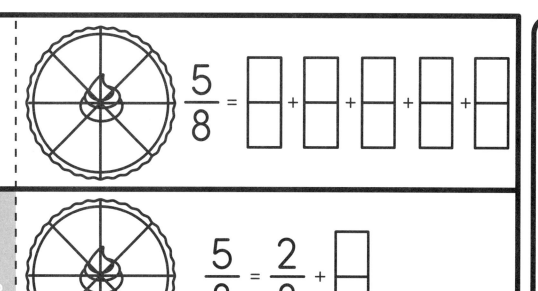

$$\frac{5}{8} = \boxed{} + \boxed{} + \boxed{} + \boxed{} + \boxed{}$$

glue

$$\frac{5}{8} = \frac{2}{8} + \boxed{}$$

glue

$$\frac{5}{8} = \frac{1}{8} + \boxed{} + \boxed{}$$

Pie Safe

Cranberry Sauce

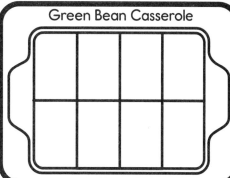

Green Bean Casserole

Snowflake Symmetry

Introduction

Before the lesson, gather or print photos of different snowflakes. Display the photos and ask students to discuss what they notice about each snowflake. Students may point out their shapes, that there are always six equal sections, and that they are each unique. Lead students to understand that snowflakes are all symmetrical and redefine the term *symmetry* if needed. If possible, it may be helpful to allow students to place mirrors on each snowflake to see the symmetry.

Creating the Notebook Page

Guide students through the following steps to complete the right-hand page in their notebooks.

1. Add a Table of Contents entry for the Snowflake Symmetry pages.

2. Cut out the title and glue it to the top of the page.

3. Cut out the *Symmetrical* and *Not Symmetrical* headers and glue them to the page below the title. Draw a vertical line to divide the center of the page into two sections.

4. Cut out the image cards. Sort them by symmetry and glue them to the correct side of the chart.

5. Cut out the snowflake grid and glue it to the bottom of the page.

6. Use what you know about symmetry to draw the other half of the snowflake. If possible, it may be helpful for students to hold up a mirror on the line of symmetry as they draw the missing half.

Reflect on Learning

To complete the left-hand page, have students create snowflakes. Give students coffee filters or cupcake liners and help them fold them into sixths. (First, fold them in half. Then, fold them in thirds.) Students should cut pieces from the folds to create symmetrical snowflakes. Glue them in the notebooks and mark the line(s) of symmetry to prove they are symmetrical.

Snowflake Symmetry

Symmetrical	Not Symmetrical

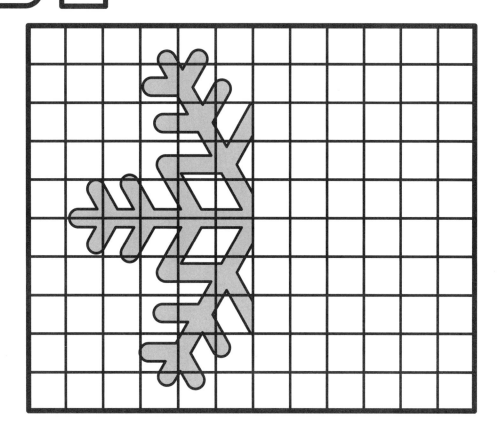

Holiday Modal Auxiliary Verbs

Introduction

Give each student a holiday bow. Ask how they would use the bow. Is it useful by itself? Discuss how a bow is meant to be used with or on something, and how it isn't useful by itself. Then, give each student a photocopy of a present. Explain that the presents are like verbs and the bows are like modal verbs—modal verbs must be paired with other verbs. Have students attach the bows to the presents and label the present *verb* and the bow *modal verb* using small sticky notes.

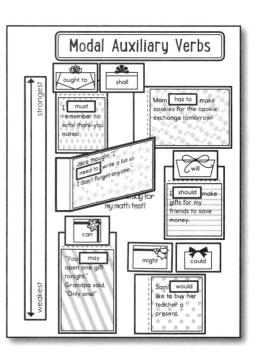

Creating the Notebook Page

Guide students through the following steps to complete the right-hand page in their notebooks.

1. Add a Table of Contents entry for the Holiday Modal Auxiliary Verbs pages.

2. Cut out the title and glue it to the top of the page.

3. Cut out the arrow piece and glue it along the left or right side of the page.

4. Cut out the six large present flaps and the six modal verb text pieces. Read each sentence and glue the best modal verb in place to complete the sentence. It may be helpful to match all of the pieces before gluing them down.

5. Cut out the six modal verb present pieces. Order the modal verb flaps and present pieces according to their degree, using the arrow piece as a guide. Apply glue to the backs of the top or left sections of the flaps and attach them to the page.

6. Under each flap, write a new sentence using the modal verb.

Reflect on Learning

To complete the left-hand page, have students write three holiday sentences using modal verbs. They should use one strong verb, one medium-strength verb, and one weak verb.

Answer Key
Strongest: ought to; shall; I **must** remember to write thank-you notes! Mom **has to** make cookies for the cookie exchange tomorrow!
Medium: will; can; I **should** make gifts for my friends to save money. Jace thought, "I **need to** write a list so I don't forget anyone."
Weakest: might; could; Sami **would** like to buy her teacher a present. "You **may** open one gift tonight," Grandpa said. "Only one!"

Modal Auxiliary Verbs

I [glue] make gifts for my friends to save money.

Sami [glue] like to buy her teacher a present.

I [glue] remember to write thank-you notes!

Mom [glue] make cookies for the cookie exchange tomorrow!

"You [glue] open one gift tonight," Grandpa said. "Only one!"

Jace thought, "I [glue] write a list so I don't forget anyone."

strongest

weakest

ought to

can

could

shall

will

might

has to

may

must

need to

should

would

Holiday Supply and Demand

Introduction

Before the lesson, gather play money and print pictures of a desirable item, such as pretend concert tickets, a homework pass, etc. Give each student play money. First, name the item and explain that you have enough of it for everyone to have one. Then, ask how much students are willing to pay for it. Record the amounts on the board. Then, set aside all but one of the items and tell students you only have one to sell. Again, ask how much students are willing to pay and record the amounts. Discuss why they were willing to pay more when there was only one available. Relate it to similar scenarios relevant to their lives, such as a library book everyone wants to read or the hot new holiday toy.

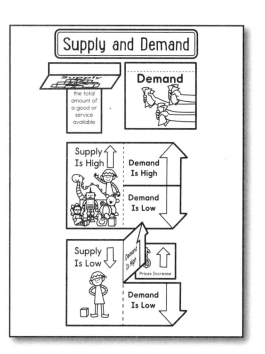

Creating the Notebook Page

Guide students through the following steps to complete the right-hand page in their notebooks.

1. Add a Table of Contents entry for the Holiday Supply and Demand pages.

2. Cut out the title and glue it to the top of the page.

3. Cut out the *Supply* and *Demand* flaps. Apply glue to the backs of the top sections and attach them to the page below the title.

4. Cut out the definition pieces and glue each one under the matching flap (Supply: the total amount of a good or service available; Demand: how interested and willing customers are to pay).

5. Cut out the *Supply Is . . .* flap books. Cut on the solid lines to create two flaps on each book. Apply glue to the backs of the left sections and attach them to the bottom of the page.

6. Cut out the *Prices Increase/Decrease* pieces. Discuss what happens during each of the four given scenarios and glue the matching piece under the flap (Supply Is High, Demand Is High: Prices Increase; Supply Is High, Demand Is Low: Prices Decrease; Supply Is Low, Demand Is High: Prices Increase; Supply Is Low, Demand Is Low: Prices Decrease). Relate supply and demand to your state's imports and exports. For example, what happens to the price of peaches when Georgia has a drought and there are fewer peaches available? Or, if there is a surplus, can that resource be exported to places that need it?

Reflect on Learning

To complete the left-hand page, have students write about current or past holiday examples of supply and demand (hot toys, etc.) using the vocabulary from the lesson.

Supply and Demand

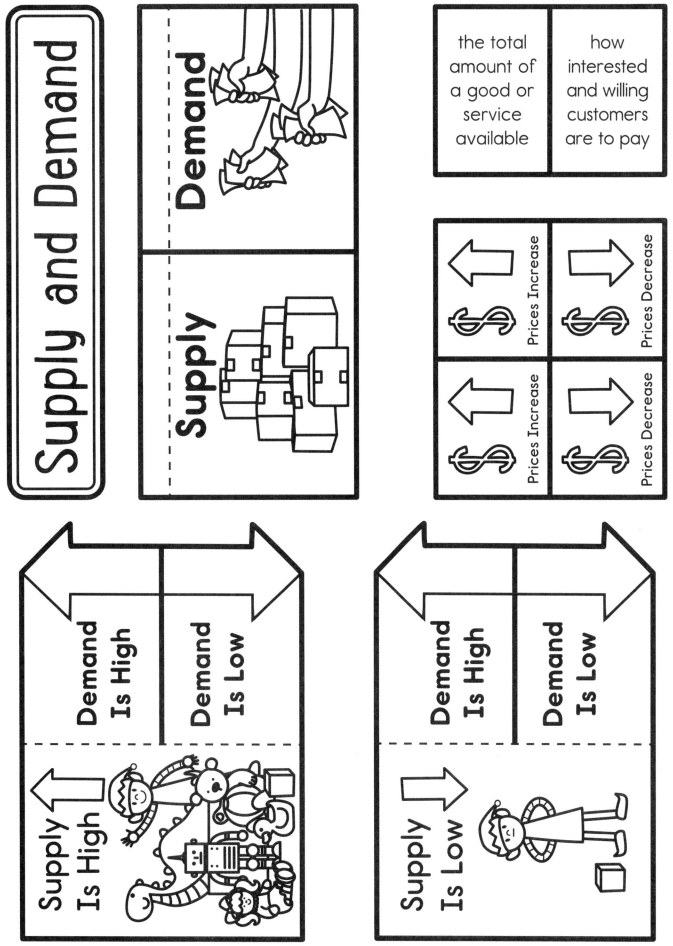

Demand

Supply

the total amount of a good or service available	how interested and willing customers are to pay

Prices Increase	Prices Increase
Prices Decrease	Prices Decrease

Demand Is High

Demand Is Low

Supply Is High

Demand Is High

Demand Is Low

Supply Is Low

New Year's Synonyms and Antonyms

Introduction

Write several words related to New Year's on the board, such as *new, fresh, beginning*, etc. As a class, work together to come up with at least one synonym and antonym for each word.

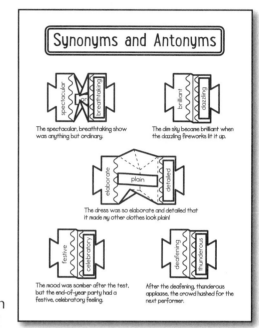

Creating the Notebook Page

Guide students through the following steps to complete the right-hand page in their notebooks.

1. Add a Table of Contents entry for the New Year's Synonyms and Antonyms pages.

2. Cut out the title and glue it to the top of the page.

3. Cut out the five firecracker pieces and the 10 word pieces. Match one synonym and one antonym to the word on each firecracker. Glue the synonym to the bottom of each piece and glue the antonym vertically in the center of the piece (it should only cross one dashed fold line). It may be helpful to match all of the pieces before gluing them down.

4. To fold each firecracker, turn it sideways so the text on each side runs vertically. Fold the two dashed vertical fold lines back and forth to create an accordion fold. The two synonym sections should meet and the points will stick out at the top and bottom. Unfold. One at a time, fold each point in toward the center by making a crease on each angled dashed line. Both points will naturally tuck in to the center of the firecracker and pull it closed. The points should now be hidden inside. When the ends of the firecrackers are pulled open and closed, the points should pop out and back in.

5. Apply glue to the back of the left section of each firecracker and attach them to the page.

6. Below or beside each firecracker, write a sentence using the words.

Reflect on Learning

To complete the left-hand page, have students write New Year's resolutions that include at least one synonym and/or antonym.

Answer Key
spectacular: S–breathtaking, A–ordinary; brilliant: S–dazzling, A–dim; festive: S–celebratory, A–somber; elaborate: S–detailed, A–plain; deafening: S–thunderous, A–hushed

Synonyms and Antonyms

breathtaking | celebratory | dazzling | detailed | dim

hushed
ordinary
plain
somber
thunderous

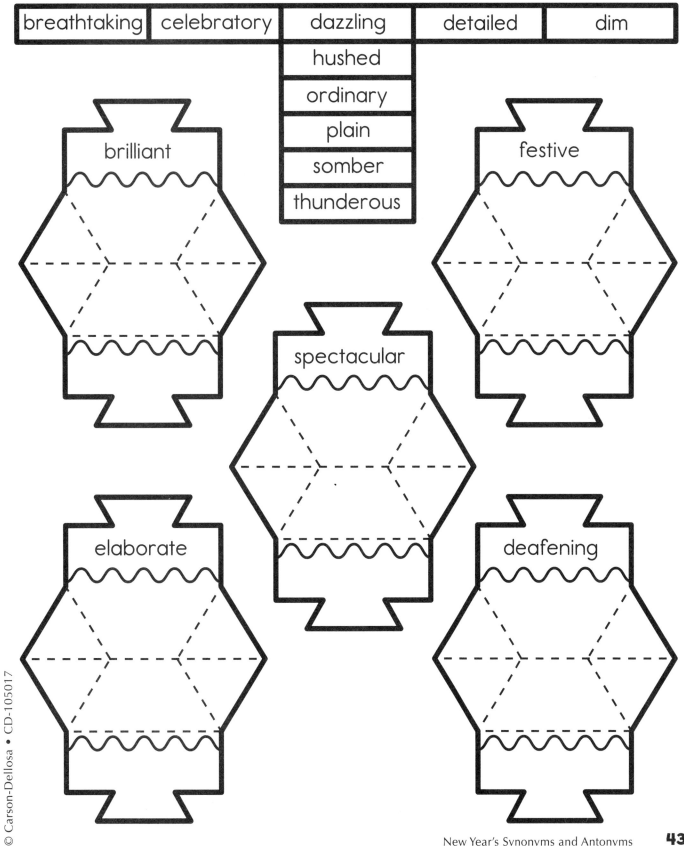

brilliant

festive

spectacular

elaborate

deafening

Black History Nonfiction Reading Comprehension

You may choose to study the passage with only the close reading activity (page 46), only the story elements activities (page 47), or both. The templates can easily be used with other nonfiction pieces.

Introduction

Read a picture book about a civil rights figure, such as Martin Luther King, Jr., Ruby Bridges, Rosa Parks, or the Greensboro Four. Allow partners to share one fact they learned from the book.

Creating the Notebook Page

Guide students through the following steps to complete the right-hand page in their notebooks.

1. Add a Table of Contents entry for the Black History Nonfiction Reading Comprehension pages.

2. Cut out the title and glue it to the top of the page.

(Not all pieces are shown.)

3. Cut out the passage (page 45) and glue it to the left-hand page. If desired, glue down only the top so it functions as a flap and the activities can be placed under the flap.

4. Cut out the flaps on page 46. Apply glue to the backs of the left sections and attach one or all to a new page.

5. Read the story each of three times. On each flap, mark how you read it, choose an area to focus on, and record your observations related to that focus. Use a different color to mark the text each time and shade the left-hand section the same color for clarity. Under each flap, write one to two sentences about the chosen focus area. For example, if main idea was chosen, you could identify the main idea and cite supporting evidence.

6. Cut out the text features pieces (page 47). Apply glue to the backs of the center sections of the *Facts* and *Main Idea* flap books and attach them to the page. Apply glue to the back of the left section of the *Key Vocabulary* flap book and attach it to the page. Glue the *Text Features* piece to the page. Apply glue to the backs of the flaps on the *Text Structure* pocket and attach it to the page. Choose the matching text structure piece, glue it to the *pull* piece, and discard the others. Slide it in the *Text Structure* pocket. Record the story elements of "Black History Month" by writing the requested information on or under each piece.

Reflect on Learning

To complete the left-hand page, have students explain the author's purpose for writing "Black History Month" and cite evidence from the text to support their answers.

Black History Month

Honoring Black History

Carter G. Woodson, the "Father of Black History"

Many agree that the beginning of equal rights for all began with President Lincoln's Emancipation Proclamation in September 1863. At that point, he declared that all slaves "shall be then, thenceforward, and forever free." From there it was still a long road to equal rights, which came to a head with the Civil Rights Movement in the 1950s and 1960s. Led by figures such as Martin Luther King, Jr., Rosa Parks, and the Little Rock Nine, black Americans began to fight for rights equal to those of white Americans.

The origins of Black History Month lie somewhere between those two important time periods. In 1915, about 50 years after the Emancipation Proclamation, Carter G. Woodson and Jesse E. Moorland founded the Association for the Study of Negro Life and History (ASNLH). Their organization was aimed at researching and publicizing the achievements of African Americans. Now known as the Association for the Study of African American Life and History (ASALH), the group promoted a national Negro History Week in 1926. They chose the second week in February because it was the same week as Abraham Lincoln's and Frederick Douglass's birthdays. During this week, communities and schools across the nation held local celebrations, performances, lectures, and other events.

From that point, mayors across the country began recognizing Negro History Week every year. As the Civil Rights Movement increased awareness, many college campuses started recognizing a Black History Month in the late 1960s instead of celebrating for only a week. It finally became a nationally recognized event in 1976, when President Gerald Ford made it official. He challenged the public to "seize the opportunity to honor the too-often neglected accomplishments of black Americans in every area of endeavor throughout our history."

Since then, every president has continued to name February as Black History Month. They choose a specific theme every year. For example, 2018's theme was "African Americans in Times of War" to celebrate the roles that black Americans have held in all American wars. The first theme, in 1928, was "Civilization: A World Achievement," while in 1976, the United States's bicentennial, it was "America for All Americans."

1st Read

I read
☐ alone.

☐ with a partner.

☐ with a group.

☐ with the teacher.

Focus
main idea(s)

key details

summary

What I Noticed
• _____

• _____

• _____

• _____

• _____

• _____

2nd Read

I read
☐ alone.

☐ with a partner.

☐ with a group.

☐ with the teacher.

Focus
vocabulary

structure of information

text features

author's purpose or point of view

What I Noticed
• _____

• _____

• _____

• _____

• _____

• _____

3rd Read

I read
☐ alone.

☐ with a partner.

☐ with a group.

☐ with the teacher.

Focus
making an inference

my opinion or connection

comparison to similar texts

What I Noticed
• _____

• _____

• _____

• _____

• _____

• _____

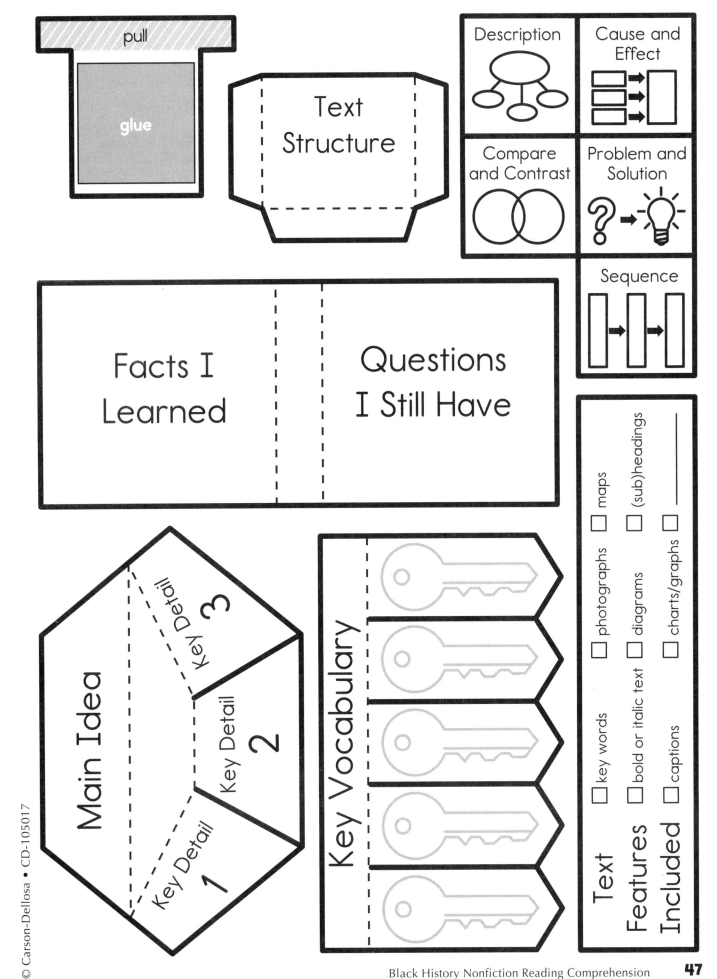

pull

glue

Text Structure

Description

Cause and Effect

Compare and Contrast

Problem and Solution

Sequence

Facts I Learned

Questions I Still Have

Main Idea

Key Detail 1

Key Detail 2

Key Detail 3

Key Vocabulary

Text Features Included

☐ maps
☐ (sub)headings
☐ photographs
☐ diagrams
☐ charts/graphs
☐ _____
☐ key words
☐ bold or italic text
☐ captions

Black History Making Inferences

Introduction

Before the lesson, find a simple puzzle—one with few and/or large pieces. Or, print a photograph and cut it into several large pieces. Give several students each a puzzle piece. Ask each student what the puzzle is a picture of. Discuss how each student's guess is based on what they can see in their pieces. Then, have students connect two pieces and allow students to revise their guesses. Continue until the puzzle is complete. Relate the puzzle pieces to background knowledge and information in a text. Explain that you put the pieces together to make inferences about the text.

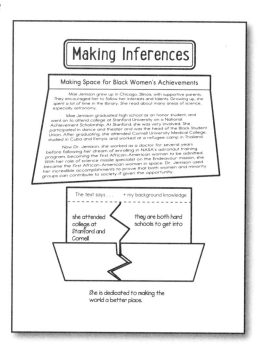

Creating the Notebook Page

Guide students through the following steps to complete the right-hand page in their notebooks.

1. Add a Table of Contents entry for the Black History Making Inferences pages.

2. Cut out the title and glue it to the top of the page.

3. Cut out the passage flap. Apply glue to the back of the top section and attach it to the page below the title.

4. Cut out one *The text says . . .* flap book. Cut on the solid lines to create two flaps. Apply glue to the back of the top section and attach it to the page under the passage flap.

5. Read the passage. As a class, make one inference about the text. Cite the text evidence on *The text says . . .* flap and your background knowledge on the *my background knowledge* flap. Under both flaps, record the inference.

6. Cut out the remaining flap books. Repeat step 4 to attach them to the bottom of the page. Then, complete two more inferences about the passage independently (or with a partner).

Reflect on Learning

To complete the left-hand page, have students write a riddle about a famous black American, ending with "Who am I?" Then, have students switch notebooks and solve the riddles, citing evidence and background knowledge that helped them infer the answer.

Making Space for Black Women's Achievements

Mae Jemison grew up in Chicago, Illinois, with supportive parents. They encouraged her to follow her interests and talents. Growing up, she spent a lot of time in the library. She read about many areas of science, especially astronomy.

Mae Jemison graduated high school as an honor student and went on to attend college at Stanford University on a National Achievement Scholarship. At Stanford, she was very involved. She participated in dance and theater and was the head of the Black Student Union. After graduating, she attended Cornell University Medical College, studied in Cuba and Kenya, and worked at a refugee camp in Thailand.

Now Dr. Jemison, she worked as a doctor for several years before following her dream of enrolling in NASA's astronaut training program, becoming the first African American woman to be admitted. With her role of science missile specialist on the *Endeavour* mission, she became the first African American woman in space. Dr. Jemison used her incredible accomplishments to prove that both women and minority groups can contribute to society if given the opportunity.

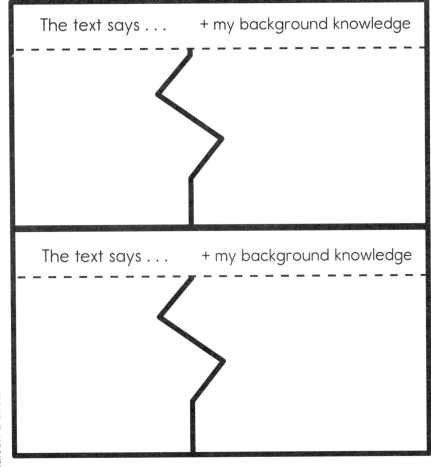

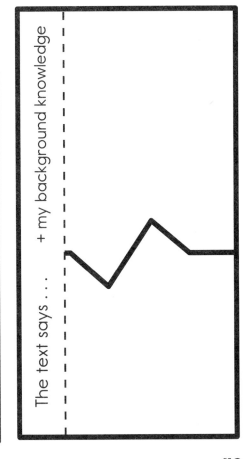

Groundhog Day Properties of Light

Students will need one brass paper fastener to complete the activity.

Introduction

Discuss Groundhog Day, Punxsutawney Phil, and the local groundhog if your state has one. Have students discuss why they think the groundhog's shadow relates to the weather and seasons. Explain that it all depends on if the day is sunny or cloudy.

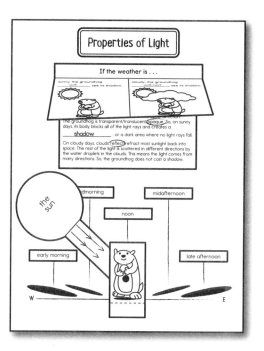

Creating the Notebook Page

Guide students through the following steps to complete the right-hand page in their notebooks.

1. Add a Table of Contents entry for the Groundhog Day Properties of Light pages.

2. Cut out the title and glue it to the top of the page.

3. Cut out the *If the weather . . .* flap book. Apply glue to the back of the top section and attach it to the page.

4. Complete the phrases on the front of each flap. (. . . sunny, the groundhog **will** see its shadow. . . . cloudy, the groundhog **will not** see its shadow.)

5. Cut out the text piece and glue it under the large flap.

6. Complete the sentences by writing or circling the correct word(s) (. . . travels in **a straight line**; The groundhog is **opaque**; . . . creates a **shadow**; . . . clouds **reflect** most sunlight . . .).

7. Cut out the groundhog, sun, and circle pieces. Place the groundhog on top, then the sun piece, and then the circle with the gray side down. Push a brass paper fastener through the dots to attach the pieces. It may be helpful to create the hole in each piece separately first. Apply glue to the gray glue section and attach it to the bottom of the page. Apply glue to the back of the bottom section of the groundhog and attach it to the page. The sun should move freely above the groundhog. Do not press the brass paper fastener through the page.

8. Draw light rays on the straight piece to show the direction of the sun's rays. Draw a horizontal line below the groundhog to represent the ground.

9. Cut out the times of day pieces. Glue them around the sun's semicircle path, like a clock, to note each time of day. Then, draw the corresponding shadow for each time. Discuss how the angle of the sun affects the shadow.

Reflect on Learning

To complete the left-hand page, have students draw diagrams showing the sun, its rays, and an opaque object to define the terms *opaque, reflect,* and *shadow.* Students should label each diagram.

Properties of Light

If the weather is . . .

sunny, the groundhog

_____ see its shadow.

cloudy, the groundhog

_____ see its shadow.

Light, including sunlight, travels in _____ .

On sunny days, the light all comes from the same direction.
The groundhog is transparent/translucent/opaque. So, on sunny
days, its body blocks all of the light rays and creates a

_____ , or a dark area where no light rays fall.

On cloudy days, clouds reflect/refract most sunlight back into
space. The rest of the light is scattered in different directions by
the water droplets in the clouds. This means the light comes from
many directions. So, the groundhog does not cast a shadow.

| early morning |
| midmorning |
| noon |
| midafternoon |
| late afternoon |

the
sun

The Reason for Four Seasons

Students will need two brass paper fasteners to complete the activity.

Introduction

Review rotation versus revolution. Explain that Earth rotates, or spins, on its axis once every 24 hours (a day). Earth revolves around the sun once every 365 days (a year). Then, have students stand in a circle. Alternately say *rotate* or *revolve*. When you say *rotate*, students should spin in place. When you say *revolve*, students should walk around the circle. Repeat several times.

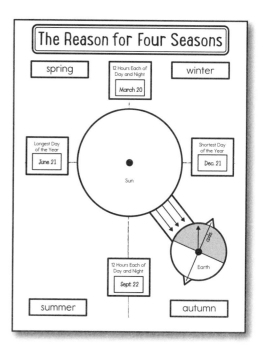

Creating the Notebook Page

Guide students through the following steps to complete the right-hand page in their notebooks.

1. Add a Table of Contents entry for The Reason for Four Seasons pages.

2. Cut out the title and glue it to the top of the page.

3. Draw horizontal and vertical lines to divide the page into quarters.

4. Cut out the *Earth* and *Sun* pieces. Label the *axis* and shade the Northern Hemisphere.

5. Cut out the gray circle and the piece with arrows. On the *Sun Here* side, place the sun on top, then the *Sun Here* piece, and then the circle with the gray side down. Push a brass paper fastener through the dots to attach the pieces. It may be helpful to create the hole in each piece separately first. Repeat the steps on the *Earth Here* side, placing the *Earth* piece on top. Apply glue to the gray glue section and attach it to the center of the page. Earth should spin freely around the sun. Do not press the brass paper fastener through the page.

6. Cut out the season pieces. Glue each piece inside the matching quarter.

7. Cut out the four equinox pieces and glue each piece in the matching quarter.

8. Write the date of each equinox for the Northern Hemisphere (Longest Day: **June 21**; Shortest Day: **December 21**; 12 Hours . . . (spring): **March 20**; 12 Hours . . . (autumn): **September 22**).

9. Hold Earth so the arrow is always pointing up and show it revolving around the sun as you discuss how the seasons are caused by the distance of the Northern Hemisphere to the sun.

Reflect on Learning

To complete the left-hand page, have students consider Australia and other countries in the Southern Hemisphere. They should use what they learned to consider when each season occurs for them. Ask, "What is the weather like during Christmas in Australia?"

The Reason for Four Seasons

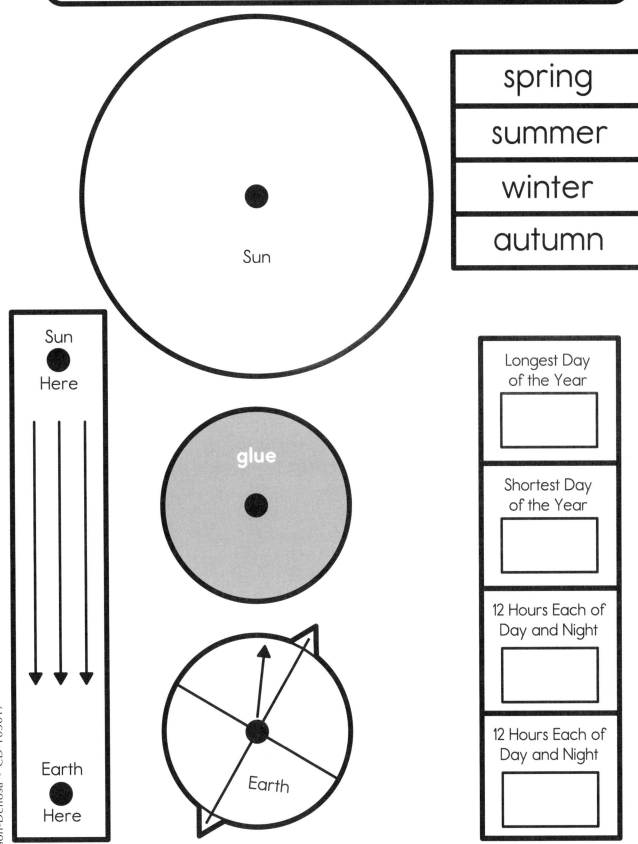

Sun

spring

summer

winter

autumn

Sun
Here

glue

Earth

Earth
Here

Longest Day of the Year

Shortest Day of the Year

12 Hours Each of Day and Night

12 Hours Each of Day and Night

Valentine's Day
Commonly Confused Words

Introduction

Read the following poem aloud: *Roses are red / But hugs are free / And kindness is sweeter / **Then** candy can **bee**. / **You're** friendship is / A generous gift. / **Their** is nothing finer— / My heart gets a lift!* Then, display the poem. Discuss what students notice. Explain that when heard, homophones don't change the meaning of a text. But, when written, homophones can change the meaning. Have students identify the homophones in the poem and correct them.

Creating the Notebook Page

Guide students through the following steps to complete the right-hand page in their notebooks.

1. Add a Table of Contents entry for the Valentine's Day Commonly Confused Words pages.

2. Cut out the title and glue it to the top of the page.

3. Cut out the trash can and mailbox pockets. Apply glue to the backs of the flaps on each and attach them side by side to the page.

4. Cut out the sentence strips. Read each one and highlight or circle each commonly confused word. There may be one or more in each sentence. Then, sort the sentences by placing the correct sentences in the mailbox and placing any sentences with errors in the trash can. Rewrite each incorrect sentence correctly on the back of the strip.

5. Draw a large tic-tac-toe grid on the bottom of the page. List each pair of commonly confused words from the sentences, placing one set in each box (hours/ours; it's/its; lose/loose; meat/meet; than/then; there/their/they're; to/two/too; whether/weather; you're/your). Add notes to help define each word.

Reflect on Learning

To complete the left-hand page, give students a copy of the following passage: *Cupid flies here, there/they're/their, and everywhere on Valentine's. His arrows are faster then/than the blink of an eye! I would like too/to/two meet/meat him and ask weather/whether he enjoys his job. I think I would/wood get board/bored the other 364 days of the year!* Have students draw a heart around the correct word(s) in each sentence.

Answer Key
Try Again: Sentences 1, 2, 4, 6, 7, 8, 9
Ready to Mail: Sentences 3, 5, 10, 11, 12

54

Commonly Confused Words

 I don't want to loose this opportunity to tell you how I feel.   1

 Its the perfect day to declare, "I love you!"   2

 You're the funniest person I know.   3

 You're eyes are like chocolate bonbons.   4

 You are more beautiful than a sunset.   5

 Their are not enough ours in the day to spend together.   6

 I cannot wait two meat you again.   7

 Let's have dinner and than see a movie.   8

 Meet me they're tonight.   9

 It's the perfect weather for a stroll outside.   10

 I don't know whether to give you flowers or candy.   11

I hope that you like me too.   12

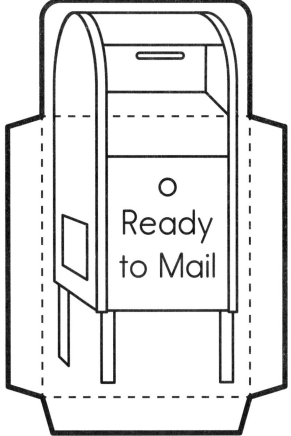

St. Patrick's Day Figurative Language

Introduction

Read or display the following saying: *May your pockets be heavy and your heart be light. May good luck pursue you each morning and night.* Ask students if it means people's pockets would be heavy, if their hearts would lose weight, or if luck would follow behind them wherever they went. Explain that the saying uses figurative language to wish people wealth, happiness, and luck. If desired, identify each type of figurative language used.

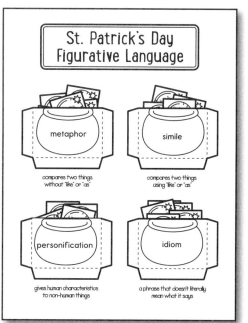

Creating the Notebook Page

Guide students through the following steps to complete the right-hand page in their notebooks.

1. Add a Table of Contents entry for the St. Patrick's Day Figurative Language pages.

2. Cut out the title and glue it to the top of the page.

3. Cut out the four pockets. Apply glue to the backs of the flaps on each pocket and attach them to the page, leaving space below each one.

4. Define each type of figurative language on the page below the pocket.

5. Cut out the gold coin pieces. Read each sentence or phrase and sort it into the correct figurative language pocket. Note: There are not equal amounts of coins for each pocket. Accept all reasonable answers. If desired, challenge students to think of more St. Patrick's Day–themed examples for other types of figurative language, such as hyperbole or alliteration.

Reflect on Learning

To complete the left-hand page, have students write their own St. Patrick's Day sentences using each of the types of figurative language listed.

Answer Key
Similes: Good friends are like four-leaf clovers—hard to find and lucky to have. She's as bright and cheerful as a rainbow. That leprechaun is as greedy as a pig! My little brother is as tricky as a leprechaun.
Metaphors: My shoes are a pot of gold—always hidden! In the sun, the dewy green shamrocks were emeralds. A horseshoe is a cup that catches luck.
Personification: Irish eyes are smiling. The pot of gold was calling her name. The clover danced in the wind.
Idioms: She has the luck of the Irish. He has more luck than sense. Don't push your luck. The third time's the charm. He has a heart of gold. This book is worth its weight in gold. All that glitters is not gold. The streets are paved with gold.

St. Patrick's Day Figurative Language

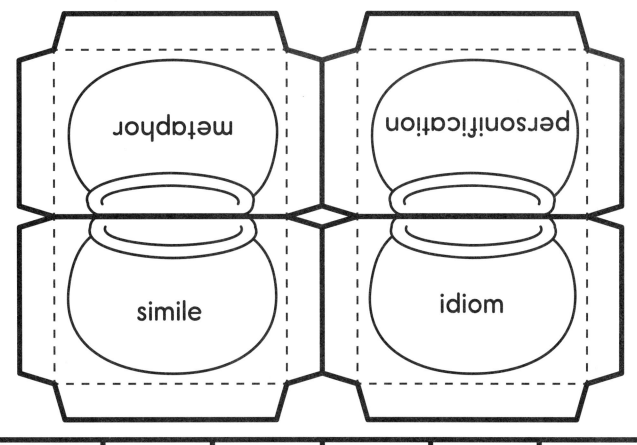

metaphor

personification

simile

idiom

Good friends are like four-leaf clovers—hard to find and lucky to have.

Irish eyes are smiling.

She has the luck of the Irish.

He has more luck than sense.

Don't push your luck.

She's as bright and cheerful as a rainbow.

The third time's the charm.

The pot of gold was calling her name.

My shoes are a pot of gold—always hidden!

That leprechaun is as greedy as a pig!

In the sun, the dewy green shamrocks were emeralds.

He has a heart of gold.

This book is worth its weight in gold.

All that glitters is not gold.

The streets are paved with gold.

The clover danced in the wind.

A horseshoe is a cup that catches luck.

My little brother is as tricky as a leprechaun.

Rainbow Factors and GCF

Introduction

Review the vocabulary for factors. Write *factor, multiple, prime, composite, greatest common factor,* and *lowest common multiple* (or any combination to match your curriculum) each on a sheet of chart paper. Place the charts around the room with a set of markers at each one. Divide students into enough groups to place a group at each chart. Have students write a definition, example, picture, etc., for the word on the chart. Then, have groups switch charts and repeat until every group has had a turn with every word. As a group, review the charts.

Creating the Notebook Page

Guide students through the following steps to complete the right-hand page in their notebooks.

1. Add a Table of Contents entry for the Rainbow Factors and GCF pages.

2. Cut out the title and glue it to the top of the page.

3. Cut out the rainbows. Apply glue to the backs of the rainbows only and attach them to the page.

4. Write the factor pairs for the given number at the bottom of each rainbow strip. Under the cloud flap, tell if the number is *prime* or *composite*. If desired, have students write the prime factorization of each number beside or below each rainbow, or on a separate sheet of paper.

5. Cut out the pots of gold flaps. Apply glue to the backs of the left sections and attach them to the bottom of the page.

6. Use the factor rainbows to identify the greatest common factor (GCF) of the two numbers given. Write the GCF under the flap.

Reflect on Learning

To complete the left-hand page, have students create their own factor rainbows for the numbers 20, 30, and 40. Then, they should find the GCF of 12 and 30 (6).

Answer Key
GCF of: 5 and 15–5; 15 and 21–3; 24 and 36–12

Factors and GCF

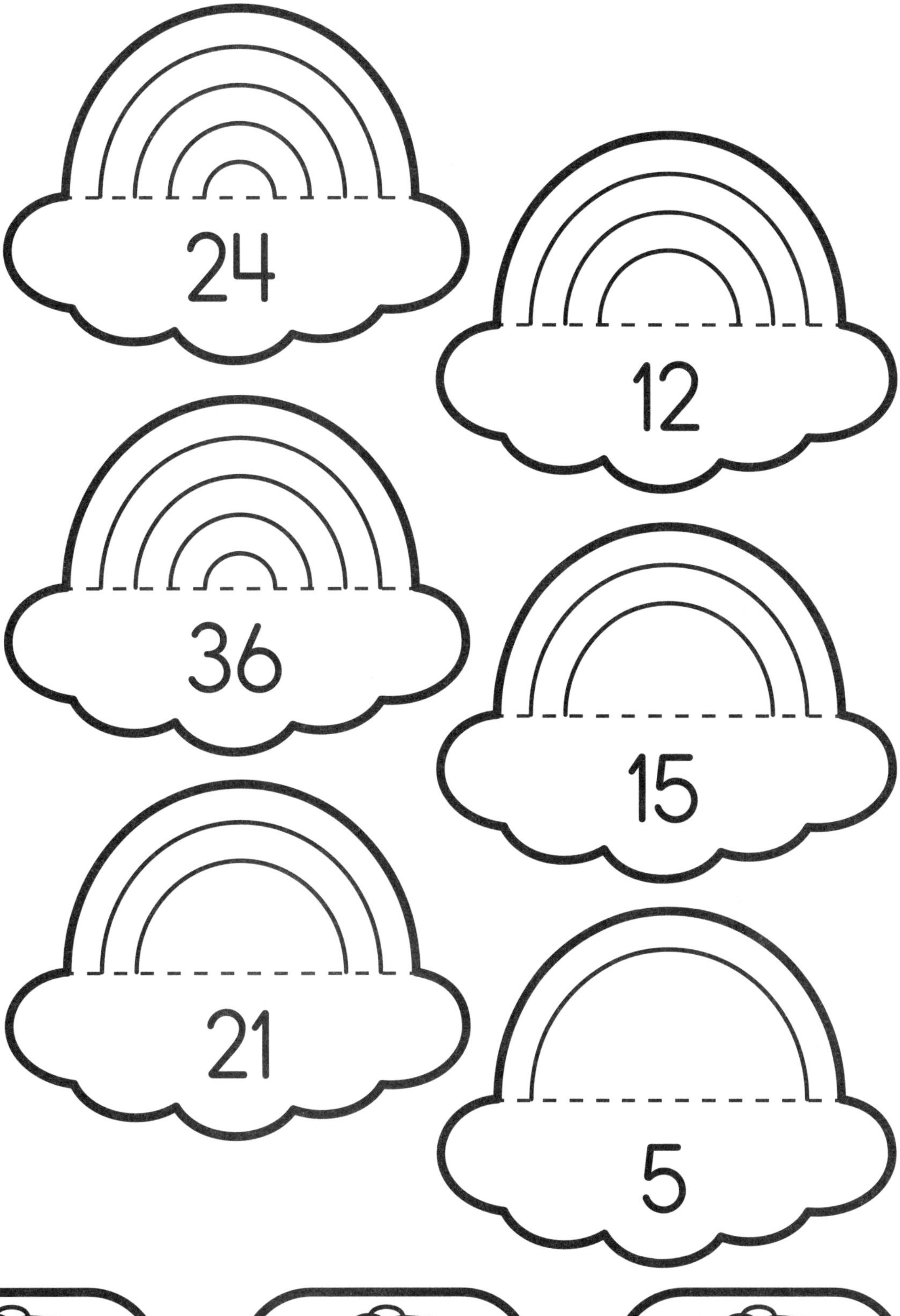
24
12
36
15
21
5

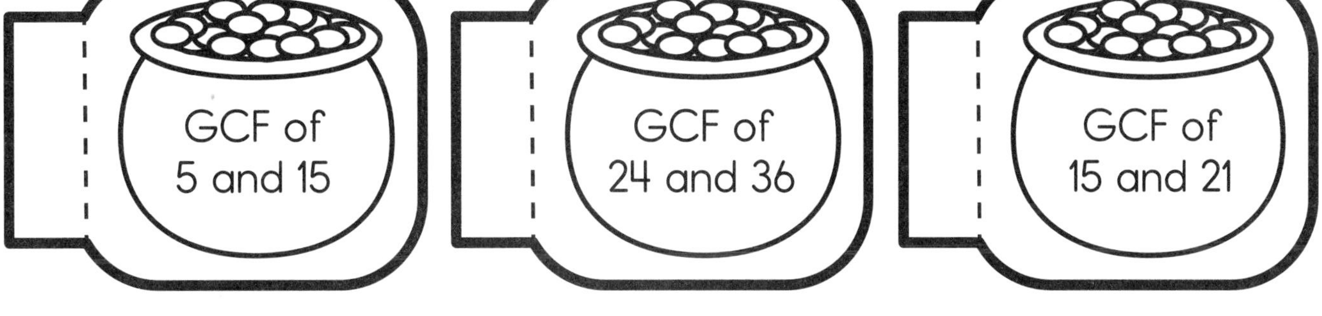
GCF of 5 and 15
GCF of 24 and 36
GCF of 15 and 21

Spring Roots and Affixes

Students will need two brass paper fasteners to complete the activity.

Introduction

Write several words with prefixes and/or suffixes on sheets of paper and display them at the front of the room. As a class, review the definitions of *root*, *base word*, *prefix*, and *suffix*. Allow students to choose a word and use scissors to cut the word apart into its word parts. Look at each part and have the class decide if it can stand alone. Discuss how roots and affixes have meaning, but they cannot stand alone. If any words included base words instead of roots (like re**view** vs. re**vise**), discuss how base words can stand alone, but adding affixes changes their meaning.

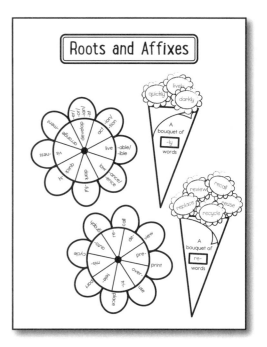

Creating the Notebook Page

Guide students through the following steps to complete the right-hand page in their notebooks.

1. Add a Table of Contents entry for the Spring Roots and Affixes pages.

2. Cut out the title and glue it to the top of the page.

3. Cut out the four circles and two flowers. Match up the prefix circle with the base word flower and the base word circle with the suffix flower. Place a circle on top, then the flower piece, and then the circle with the gray side down. Push a brass paper fastener through the dots to attach the pieces. It may be helpful to create the hole in each piece separately first. Repeat with the other set of pieces to create two flower spinners. Apply glue to the gray glue section of the circles and attach them to the page. The flower and affix circle should spin freely. Do not press the brass paper fastener through the page.

4. Cut out the *A bouquet of . . .* pieces and glue them to the bottom or side of the page.

5. Choose a prefix and suffix and write them on the bouquet pieces. Spin each spinner to match up roots or base words with each affix. Record each new word above the matching bouquet piece. If desired, add a flower design around each word.

Reflect on Learning

To complete the left-hand page, have students list and define as many words as they can using the roots, bases, and affixes on the right-hand page. Students may include additional roots and affixes that are not included, as long as the final word includes a word part from the right-hand page.

Roots and Affixes

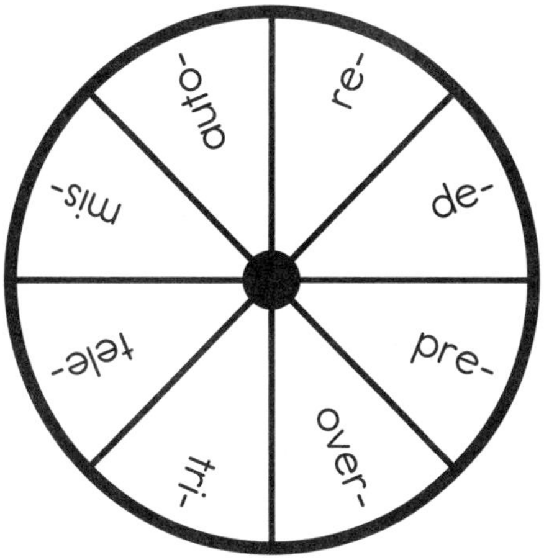

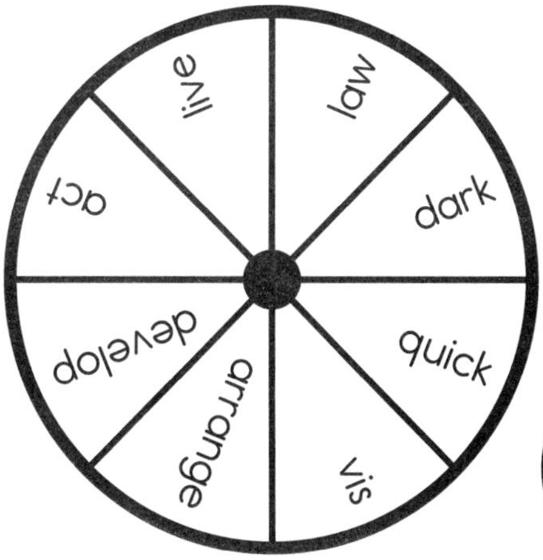

Spinner 1 (prefixes):
- re-
- de-
- pre-
- over-
- tri-
- tele-
- mis-
- auto-

Spinner 2 (roots):
- may
- dark
- quick
- vis
- arrange
- develop
- act 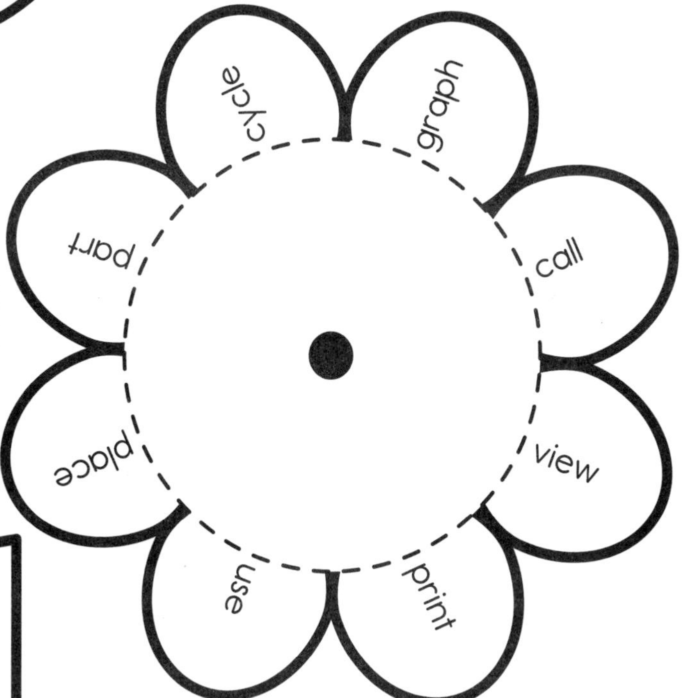
- liv

glue

glue

Flower 1 (roots):
- cycle
- graph
- call
- view
- print
- use
- place
- part

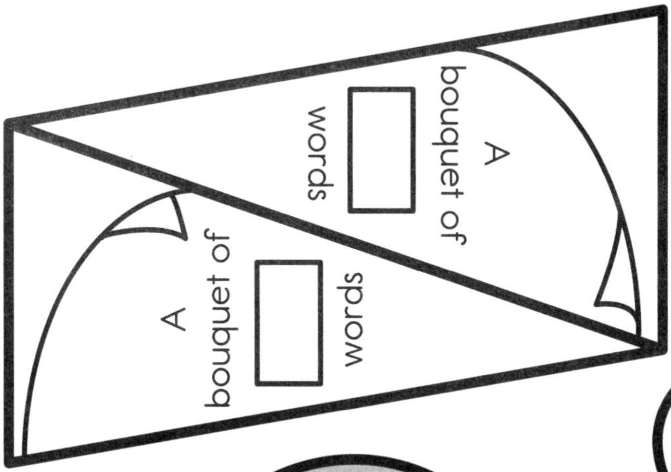

Flower 2 (suffixes):
- -ance / -ence
- -ful
- -ly
- -ness
- -ment
- -er / -or / -ian / -ist
- -ion / -tion
- -able / -ible

A bouquet of [ ] words

A bouquet of [ ] words

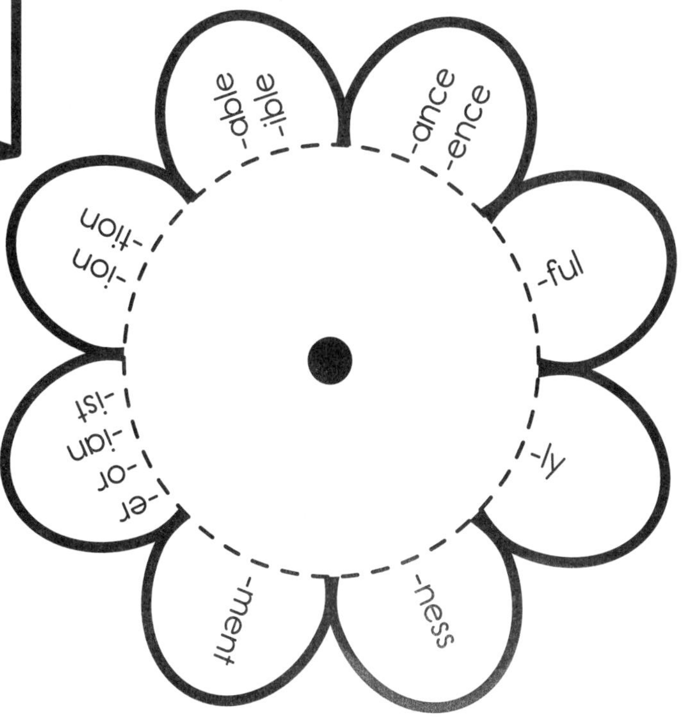

Measuring Angles of Sunrays

Students will need a brass paper fastener and a protractor to complete the activity.

Introduction

Review angle basics. Have students hold up both hands, touching over their heads. Then, direct them to move one arm around in a circle to show the 360 degrees in a circle. Then, have them move one arm to show 90°, 180°, and 270° (keeping one arm pointing up at 0° the whole time). Then, have students put their arms down. Name different angle types, such as acute, right, obtuse, straight, etc., and have students use their arms to show the matching angle.

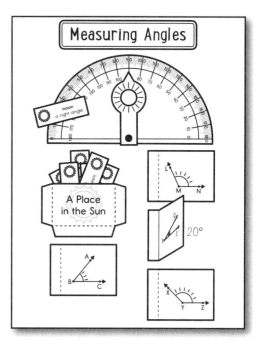

Creating the Notebook Page

Guide students through the following steps to complete the right-hand page in their notebooks.

1. Add a Table of Contents entry for the Measuring Angles of Sunrays pages.

2. Cut out the title and glue it to the top of the page.

3. Cut out the protractor and the sun arrow piece. Place the sun piece on top of the protractor. Push a brass paper fastener through the dots to attach the pieces. It may be helpful to create the hole in each piece separately first. Glue the protractor to the page below the title. The sun piece should move freely. Do not press the brass paper fastener through the page.

4. Cut out the *A Place in the Sun* pocket. Apply glue to the backs of the flaps and attach it to the page.

5. Cut out the ten time-of-day cards and store them in the pocket.

6. Pull out a time-of-day card and model the angle given on the protractor.

7. Cut out the angle flaps. Apply glue to the backs of the left sections and attach them to the page.

8. Use a protractor to measure each angle. Write the angle measure under the flap.

Reflect on Learning

To complete the left-hand page, have students use rulers to draw a box with several straight lines intersecting the box. Then, students should use a protractor to measure several of the angles created and mark each angle with its measure.

Answer Key
∠ABC: 50°; ∠LMN: 115°; ∠QRS: 20°; ∠XYZ: 135°

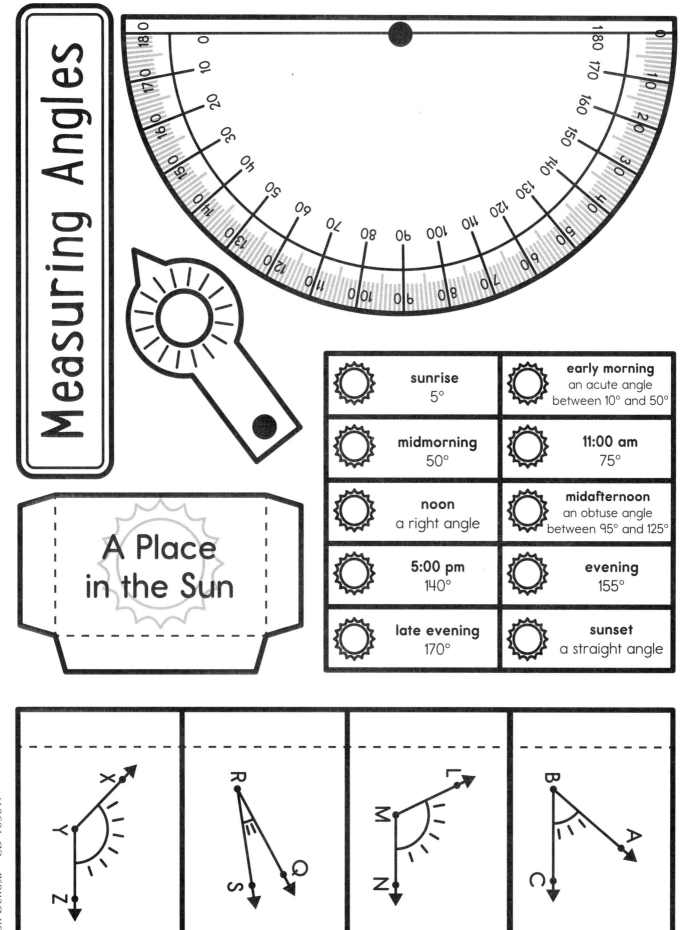

Measuring Angles

A Place in the Sun

sunrise 5°	**early morning** an acute angle between 10° and 50°
midmorning 50°	**11:00 am** 75°
noon a right angle	**midafternoon** an obtuse angle between 95° and 125°
5:00 pm 140°	**evening** 155°
late evening 170°	**sunset** a straight angle

Earth Day Vocabulary

Introduction

Remind students that Earth Day, April 22, promotes environmental awareness across the globe. Draw a large heart on the board. Ask students what Earth Day means to them and for ways they celebrate it. Record their thoughts inside the heart.

Creating the Notebook Page

Guide students through the following steps to complete the right-hand page in their notebooks.

1. Add a Table of Contents entry for the Earth Day Vocabulary pages.

2. Cut out the title and glue it to the top of the page.

3. Cut out the heart piece. Do not cut on the solid line to separate hearts 1 and 4 yet. Fold the piece in half vertically and horizontally on the dashed fold lines (it will also fold on the cut line between hearts 1 and 4). Then, fold the piece in half diagonally in both directions (through the text). There should be four complete folds through the entire piece. Cut on the solid line between hearts 1 and 4.

4. Glue the backs of adjacent heart halves together. So, glue the back right side of heart 1 to the back left side of heart 2; the back right side of heart 2 to the back left side of heart 3; and the back right side of heart 3 to the back left side of heart 4. Glue the remaining left side of heart 1 and the right side of heart 4 to the page. It should create a heart-shaped booklet with four pages.

5. Cut out the four vocabulary flaps. Apply glue to the backs of the top sections and attach them to the page below the heart booklet.

6. Read the passage in the heart booklet. On each page, use the context clues to determine the meaning of the bold word. Write a short definition of that word on its flap. Under the flap, write the context clues that helped you determine the meaning.

Reflect on Learning

To complete the left-hand page, have students create an Earth Day poster promoting the holiday using one or more facts from the passage.

Earth Day Vocabulary

spew	spotlight	establish	safeguard
means	means	means	means
because . . .	because . . .	because . . .	because . . .

The Origins of Earth Day

It may be difficult to imagine now, but before 1970, factories could legally dump chemicals into rivers or **spew** toxic clouds into the air. Smog and pollution were common and large cars ran on leaded gas. But, the public was slowly beginning to see the link between pollutants and the health of the environment.

After a major oil spill in California, Sen. Gaylord Nelson decided to increase awareness about the environment. He played a major part in organizing demonstrations and rallies across the country on April 22, 1970. He hoped to push environmental responsibility into the public and political **spotlight.**

About 20 million Americans participated in the first Earth Day. By the end of 1970, changes had begun. The Environmental Protection Agency was **established.** The Clean Air Act, the Endangered Species Act, and several other environmental laws had been passed.

Since 1970, Earth Day has blossomed. In some places, it has even become Earth Week. It has grown to include over 140 nations. According to the Earth Day Network, over one billion people participate in Earth Day activities. Earth Day has united the world in **safeguarding** the environment.

1 2
4 3

Poetry Month Elements of Poetry

Because the poem provided is old, it includes some difficult language. The Introduction activity is intended to pre-teach and reinforce the new vocabulary.

Introduction

Before the lesson, write each of the following vocabulary words on a card along with a simple definition for each: *woes, prose, blight, cipher, heed, vow, cast, bough, giddy, frigid.* Divide students into 10 groups and give each group a large sheet of paper and a vocabulary word card. They should read the definition, write the word, and draw a clear and simple related picture. For example, for *heed,* students might draw an ear or an object with many arrows pointing toward it. Allow each group to share their word, definition, and drawing. Display the drawings during this lesson. Encourage students to refer to the posters throughout the activity.

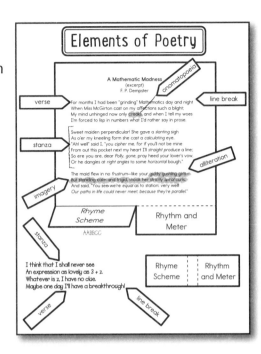

Creating the Notebook Page

Guide students through the following steps to complete the right-hand page in their notebooks.

1. Add a Table of Contents entry for the Poetry Month Elements of Poetry pages.

2. Cut out the title and glue it to the top of the page.

3. Cut out the poem flap book. Cut on the solid line to create two flaps. Apply glue to the back of the poem section and attach it to the page.

4. Cut out one set of poetry elements arrow pieces. Color each one a different color.

5. Read the poem. Then, reread it, looking for each poetry element. Once you find an example of each, circle or highlight the text in the same color and glue the arrow nearby. Repeat until all elements have been identified. Note: some elements may appear multiple times. You may choose to highlight one or all. Determine the rhyme scheme and if the poem has rhythm and meter, and record each under the correct flap.

6. At the bottom of the page or on a new page, write your own short, silly poem.

7. Cut out the second set of arrow pieces and the *Rhyme Scheme* flap book. Apply glue to the back of the center section and attach it to the page near your poem. Repeat step 5 to label the elements of your poem.

Reflect on Learning

To complete the left-hand page, have students describe how the poem would be affected if one element was removed, such as the rhyme scheme or alliteration.

Elements of Poetry

A Mathematic Madness
(excerpt)
F. P. Dempster

For months I had been "grinding" Mathematics day and night
When Miss McGirton cast on my affections such a blight;
My mind unhinged now only creaks, and when I tell my woes
I'm forced to lisp in numbers what I'd rather say in prose.

Sweet maiden *perpendicular*! She gave a *slanting* sigh
As o'er my kneeling form she cast a *calculating* eye.
"Ah! well" said I, "you *cipher* me, for if you'll not be mine
From out this pocket next my heart I'll *straight produce a line*;
So ere you are, dear *Polly*, *gone*, pray heed your lover's vow,
Or he dangles at *right angles* to some *horizontal* bough."

The maid flew in no *frustrum*—like your giddy gushing girls—
But standing calm and frigid, shook her strictly *spiral* curls,
And said, "You see we're *equal* as to station: very well!
Our paths in life could never meet, because they're parallel."

Rhyme Scheme	Rhythm and Meter

Rhythm and Meter

Rhyme Scheme

imagery	imagery
stanza	stanza
verse	verse
line break	line break
onomatopoeia	onomatopoeia
alliteration	alliteration

Local Traditions and Celebrations

Before copying page 69, choose six festivals and celebrations unique to your state and write one on each flap of the bottom piece, leaving space for students to draw a symbol. Write your state's name in the center.

Introduction

Explain that there are only 10 federal holidays, but states can create and celebrate their own public holidays, although state and federal holidays often overlap. For example, Texas celebrates Juneteenth and Texas Independence Day, and California celebrates Cesar Chavez Day. States may also have other festivals and celebrations to celebrate local history and resources. For example, Lexington, North Carolina, holds a barbeque festival to celebrate their nationally known pork barbeque, and Oak Forest, Illinois, celebrates Irish heritage with the Gaelic Park Irish Fest. Have students brainstorm a list of local holidays, traditions, and celebrations.

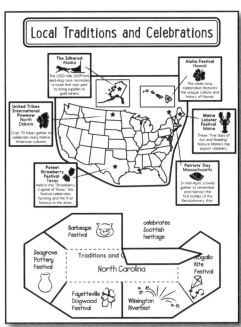

Creating the Notebook Page

Guide students through the following steps to complete the right-hand page in their notebooks.

1. Add a Table of Contents entry for the Local Traditions and Celebrations pages.

2. Cut out the title and glue it to the top of the page.

3. Cut out the map and glue it to the page, leaving some space above it.

4. Cut out the six festival pieces. Read about each unique festival, locate its star on the map, and glue it nearby. Draw a line from the description to its spot on the map. Discuss how local traditions and celebrations often celebrate unique local culture, history, or resources.

5. Cut out the flap book. Cut on the solid lines to create six flaps. Apply glue to the back of the center section and attach it to the bottom of the page.

6. On each flap, draw a symbol for that festival or celebration. Under the flap, write a short description, including how it is connected to local history, culture, resources, etc.

Reflect on Learning

To complete the left-hand page, provide a list of local and state festivals, celebrations, etc. Have students choose one to research and report on by making a poster, brochure, or short presentation of your choosing.

Local Traditions and Celebrations

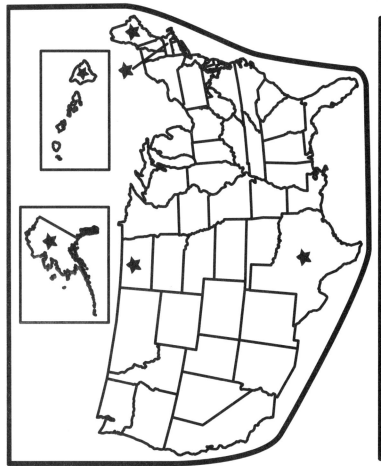

The Iditarod
Alaska

This 1,000-mile (1,609 km) sled-dog race recreates a route that was used to bring supplies to gold miners.

Aloha Festival
Hawaii

This week-long celebration features the unique culture and history of Hawaii.

Maine Lobster Festival
Maine
These "five days of fun and feasting" feature Maine's top export—lobsters.

Patriots' Day
Massachusetts

In mid-April, crowds gather to remember and reenact the first battles of the Revolutionary War.

United Tribes International Powwow
North Dakota
Over 70 tribes gather to celebrate many Native American cultures.

Poteet Strawberry Festival
Texas
Held in the "Strawberry Capital of Texas," this festival celebrates farming and the fruit famous to the area.

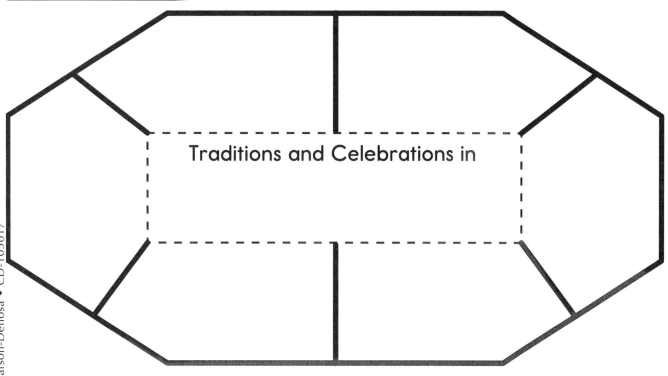

Traditions and Celebrations in

Equivalent Ice-Cream Cones

Introduction

Before the lesson, hang a length of yarn or clothesline across the front of the room. Tape an index card with *0* written on it to the left side and a card with *1* written on it to the right side. Collect enough clothespins or clips for each student to have one. Give each student a clothespin and a sticky note. Have students write any fraction or decimal less than 1 on their sticky notes. Allow students to approach the number line and add their fraction or decimal in the correct place. For students who have chosen the same number, create a vertical chain of clips. Discuss how students were able to place both fractions and decimals on the same number line, and how they knew where to place them.

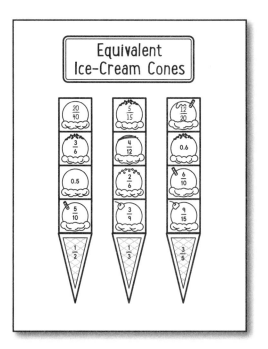

Creating the Notebook Page

Guide students through the following steps to complete the right-hand page in their notebooks.

1. Add a Table of Contents entry for the Equivalent Ice-Cream Cones pages.

2. Cut out the title and glue it to the top of the page.

3. Cut out the ice-cream cones and glue them across the bottom of the page. You will have to use two pages, so either use a full spread (left-hand and right-hand pages) or use two right-hand pages in a row.

4. Cut out the ice-cream scoops, leaving the row of blank scoops together. Place the blank scoops aside. Sort the fraction and decimal scoops above the equivalent fraction ice-cream cone. Once all of the scoops have been sorted, glue the scoops above each cone.

5. Cut apart the blank ice-cream scoops. Glue each one to the top of each set of ice-cream scoops and write your own equivalent fraction on the scoop.

Reflect on Learning

To complete the left-hand page, have students explain how they knew 0.6 was equivalent to 3/5.

Answer Key
1/2: 0.5; 3/6; 5/10
1/3: 3/9; 2/6; 4/12
1/4: 0.25; 2/8; 25/100
2/10: 0.2; 1/5; 20/100
3/4: 0.75; 75/100; 9/12
3/5: 0.6; 6/10; 9/15

Equivalent Ice-Cream Cones

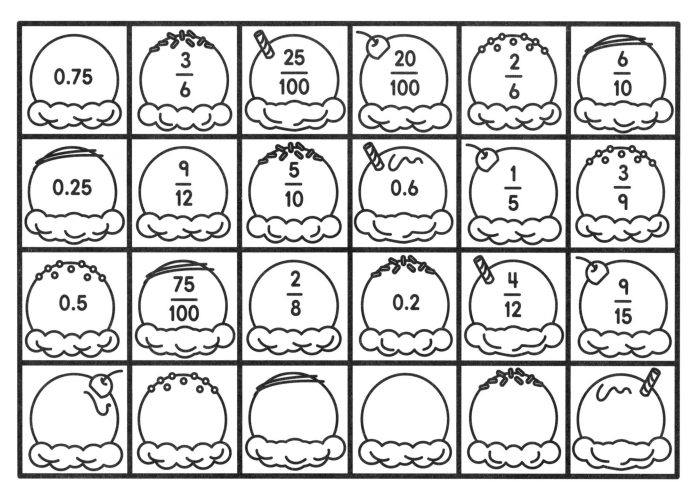

0.75	$\frac{3}{6}$	$\frac{25}{100}$	$\frac{20}{100}$	$\frac{2}{6}$	$\frac{6}{10}$
0.25	$\frac{9}{12}$	$\frac{5}{10}$	0.6	$\frac{1}{5}$	$\frac{3}{9}$
0.5	$\frac{75}{100}$	$\frac{2}{8}$	0.2	$\frac{4}{12}$	$\frac{9}{15}$

$\frac{1}{2}$	$\frac{1}{3}$	$\frac{1}{4}$
$\frac{3}{5}$	$\frac{3}{4}$	$\frac{2}{10}$

US and State Symbols

Introduction

Give each student two sticky notes. Have students draw the first thing they think of when you say *Independence Day* or *Fourth of July.* Have students place their personal symbols on the board. Define and discuss symbols. For example, the American flag is often used on Independence Day to represent the country and the celebration of its beginnings. Repeat the activity with *United States* or *America.* Discuss the country's symbols. Explain that each state also has its own symbols.

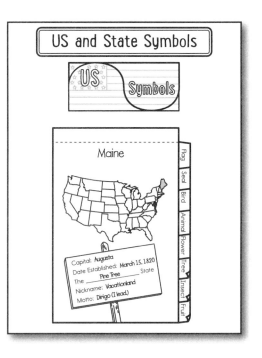

Creating the Notebook Page

Guide students through the following steps to complete the right-hand page in their notebooks.

1. Add a Table of Contents entry for the US and State Symbols pages.

2. Cut out the title and glue it to the top of the page.

3. Cut out the *US Symbols* piece. Cut the two short, solid lines. Fold the flaps in on the dashed lines to close the booklet. Apply glue to the gray glue section and attach it to the page.

4. Cut out the six US symbol pieces and glue them inside the booklet. Discuss the symbols. If desired, share additional symbols not included and note or sketch them inside the booklet.

5. Cut out the nine large flaps (pages 73–77). Discard any flaps that do not apply to your state (for example, not all states have an official insect). Apply glue to the gray glue sections and stack the flaps to create a stacked flap book of nine (or fewer) pages. In order from front to back, the pages are cover, *Flag, Seal, Bird, Animal, Flower, Tree, Insect,* and *Fruit.* Apply glue to the back of the top section and attach it to the bottom of the page. It may be useful to glue two pages in your notebook together to create a reinforced page to support the flap book.

6. On each page of the stacked flap book, complete any prompts or pictures. On the blank pages, name the symbol and draw a picture. On the *Animal* flap, include any state animals, such as state mammal, cat, dog, etc. You may use extra page space to add additional notes about the symbol, such as why it's relevant to your state, when it was added, interesting details, etc. On the notebook page behind the final flap, include any other symbols not covered by the flap book, such as the state song, reptile, shell, fish, gemstone, etc.

Reflect on Learning

To complete the left-hand page, look at symbols that other states have that your state doesn't. Have students choose one of those symbols and write a letter to a senator stating their choice for that symbol and explaining why they chose it to represent their state.

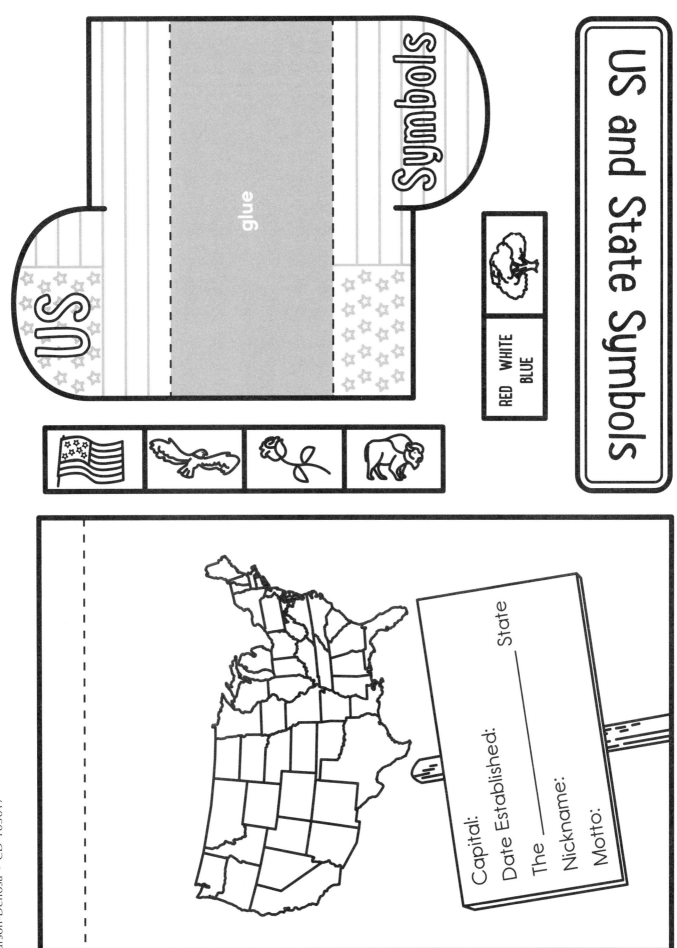

US

Symbols

glue

RED   WHITE
BLUE

US and State Symbols

State

Capital:
Date Established:
The _____ Nickname:
Motto:

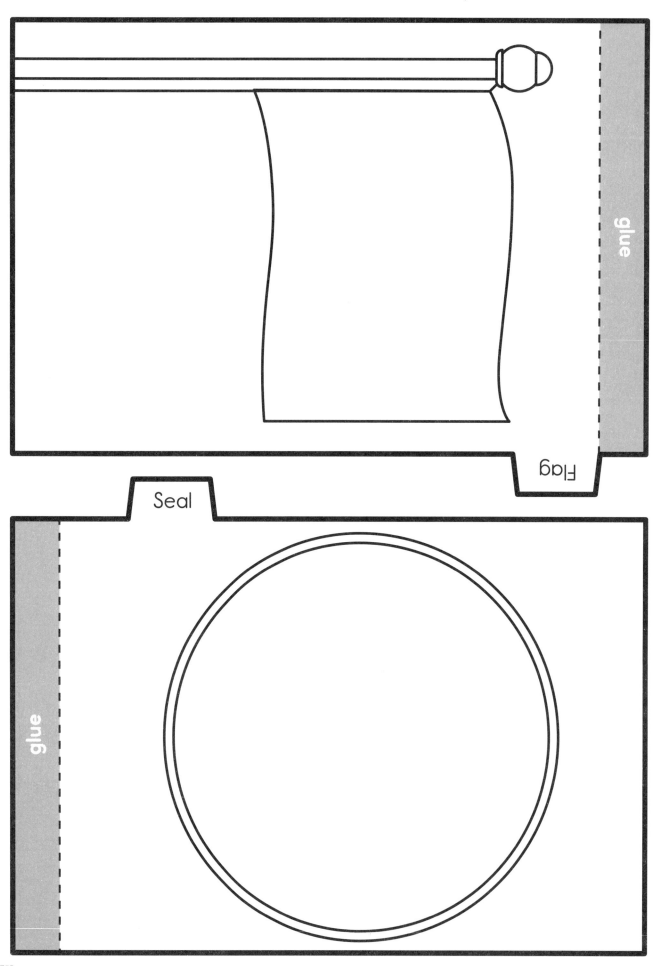

glue

Flag

Seal

glue

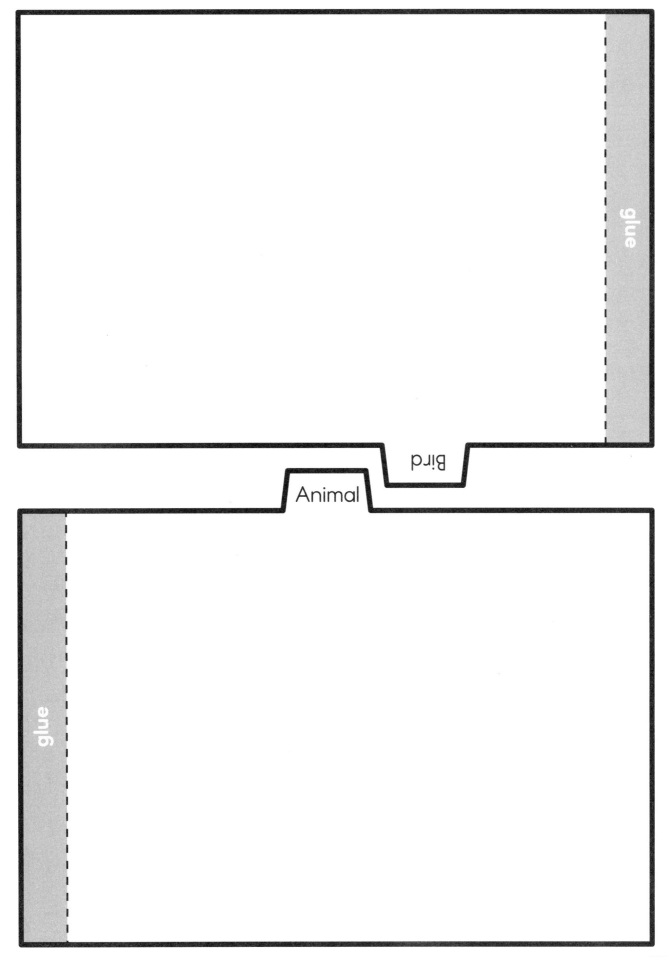

glue

Bird

Animal

glue

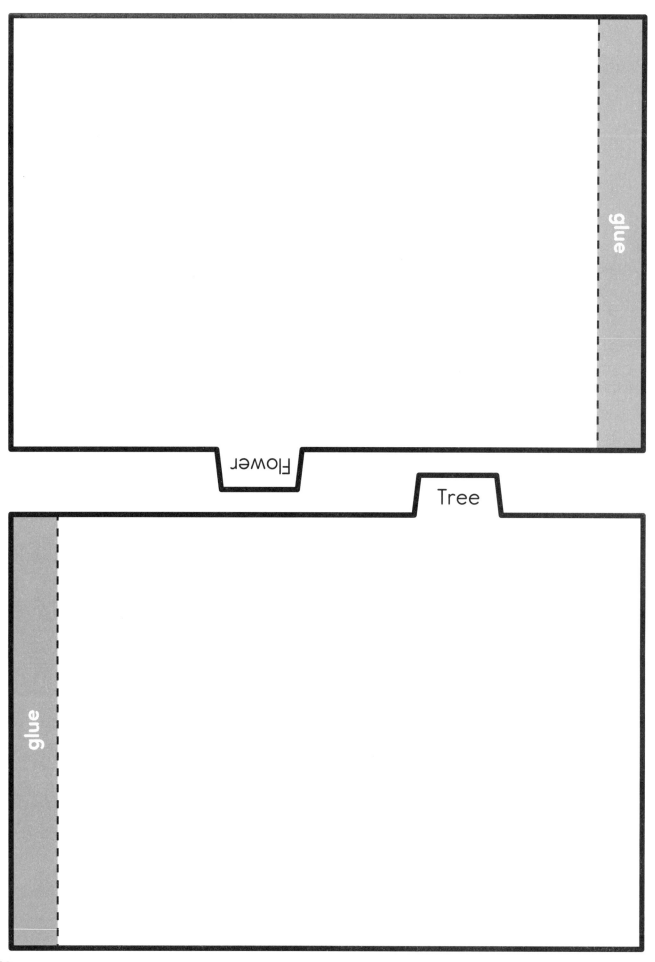

glue

Flower

Tree

glue

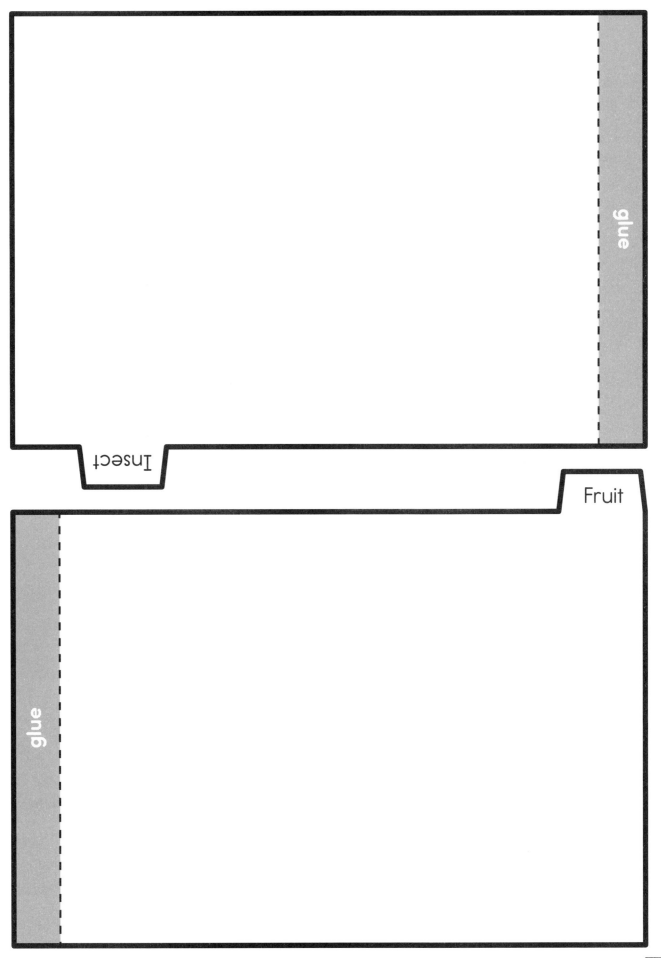

glue

Insect

Fruit

glue

glue

Apple and Leaf Accordion Folds

Cut out the accordion pieces on the solid lines. Fold on the dashed lines, alternating the fold direction. Apply glue to the back of the last section to attach it to a notebook page.

You may modify the accordion books to have more or fewer pages by cutting off extra pages or by having students glue the first and last panels of two accordion books together.

78

Pumpkin Flaps

Cut out each pumpkin flap. Apply glue to the back of the narrow section to attach it to a notebook page.

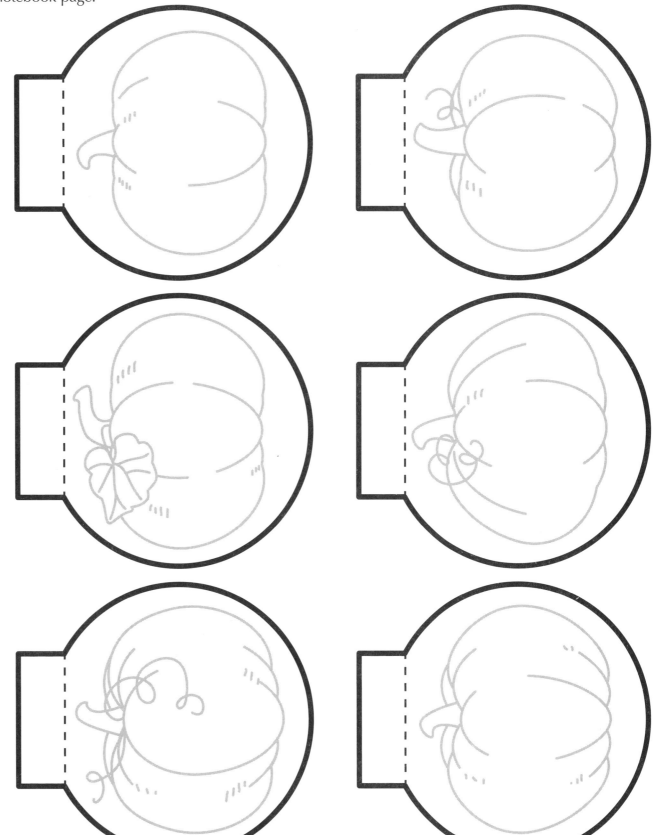

Spiderweb Petal Fold

Cut out the spiderweb on the solid lines. Cut on the solid lines to create six flaps. Then, fold the flaps toward the center and back out. Apply glue to the back of the center panel to attach it to a notebook page.

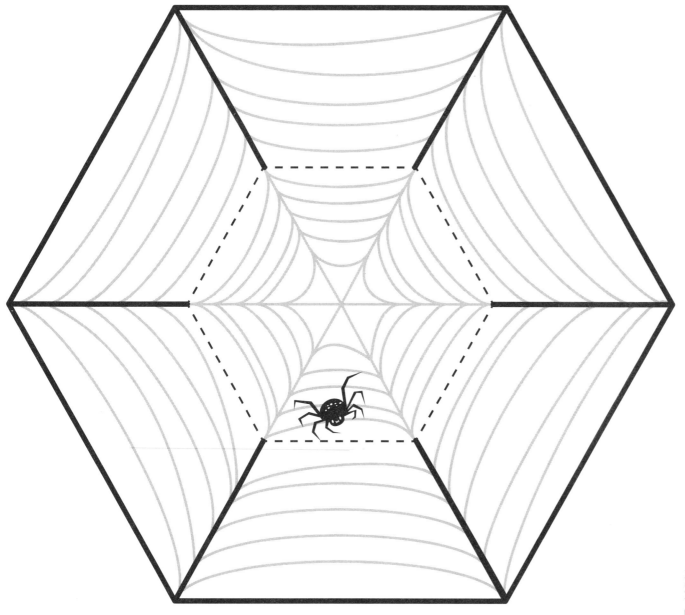

Candy Corn Flap Books

Cut out the flap books around the outside borders. Then, cut on the solid lines to create three flaps on each book. Apply glue to the backs of the left sections to attach them to a notebook page.

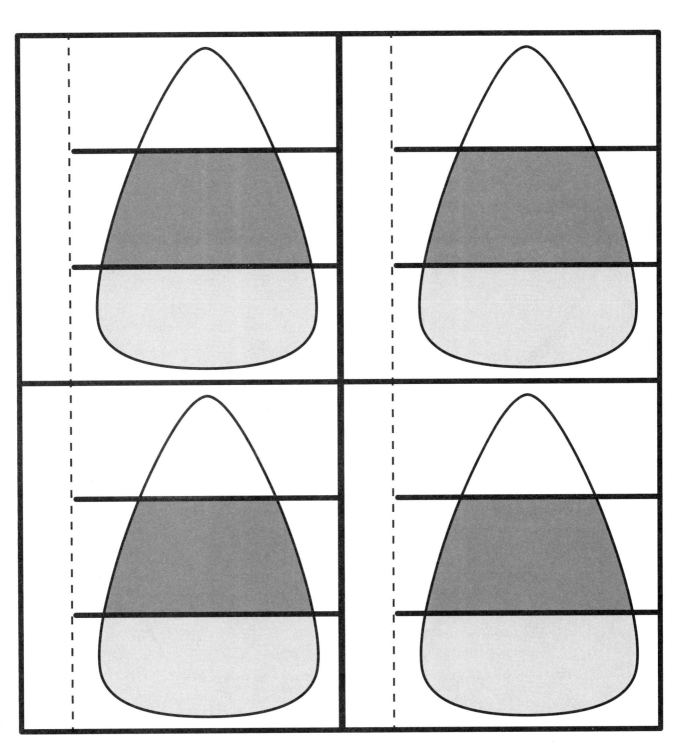

Turkey Flap Book

Cut out the flap book around the outside borders. Then, cut on the solid lines to create separate feather flaps. Apply glue to the back of the turkey body to attach it to a notebook page.

Cornucopia Pocket

Cut out the cornucopia on the solid lines. Apply glue to the backs of the six narrow sections and attach it to a notebook page. Cut out the fruit, vegetable, and plant pieces and place them in the cornucopia pocket.

Snowflake Petal Fold

Cut out the snowflake on the solid lines. Cut on the solid lines to create six flaps. Then, fold the flaps toward the center and back out. Apply glue to the back of the center panel to attach it to a notebook page.

Snowmen Flap Books

Cut out the flap books around the outside borders. Then, cut on the solid lines to create three flaps on each book. Apply glue to the backs of the left sections to attach them to a notebook page.

Tree and Ornament Flaps

Cut out the tree and glue it to a notebook page. Cut out each ornament flap. Apply glue to the back of the top section to attach it to the notebook page on and around the tree.

Fireworks Petal Folds

Cut out the fireworks on the solid lines. Cut on the solid lines to create five flaps on each firework. Then, fold the flaps toward the centers and back out. Apply glue to the backs of the center panels to attach them to a notebook page.

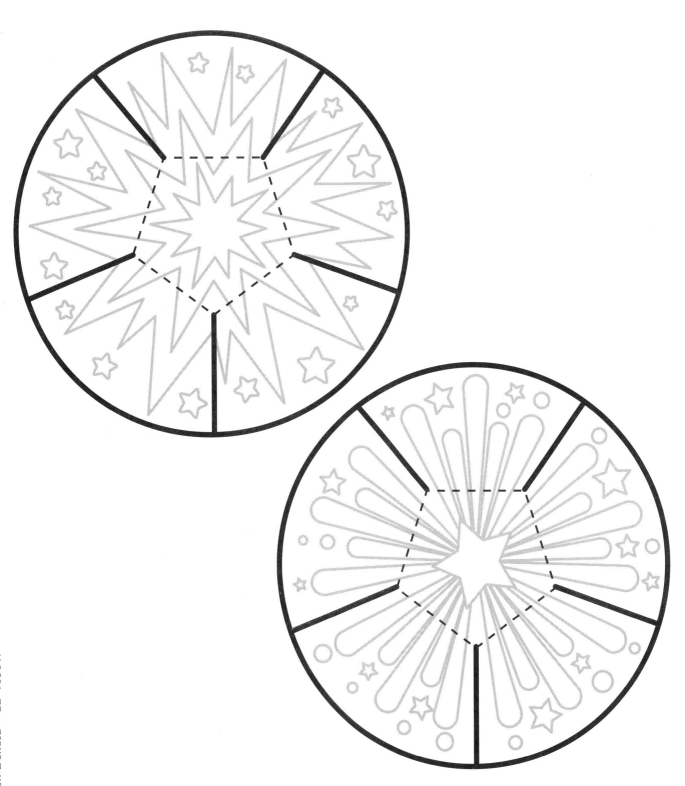

New Year's Eve Accordion Folds

Cut out the accordion pieces on the solid lines. Fold the left and right sides toward the center on the dashed lines, alternating the fold direction. Apply glue to the back of the left section to attach it to a notebook page.

Valentine's Day Envelope and Letters

Cut out the envelope on the solid lines. Apply glue to the backs of the three narrow sections and attach it to a notebook page. Cut out the blank letter pieces and place them in the envelope.

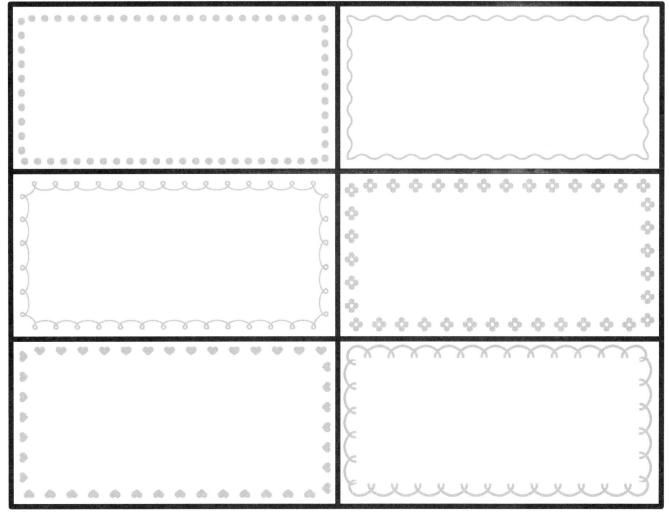

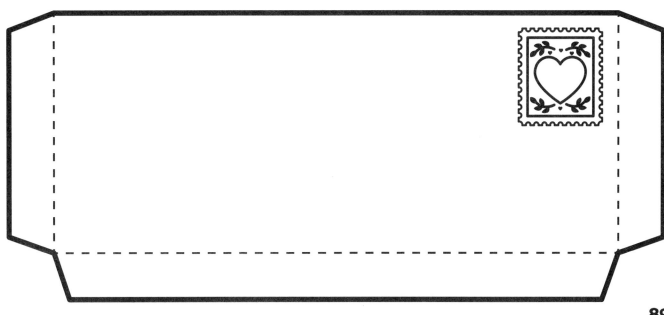

Heart Flaps

Cut out each heart flap. Apply glue to the back of the narrow section to attach it to a notebook page.

Rainbow and Pot o' Gold Flaps

Cut out the rainbow and glue it to the notebook page. Cut out each pot o' gold flap. Apply glue to the back of the narrow section to attach it to the notebook page near the rainbow.

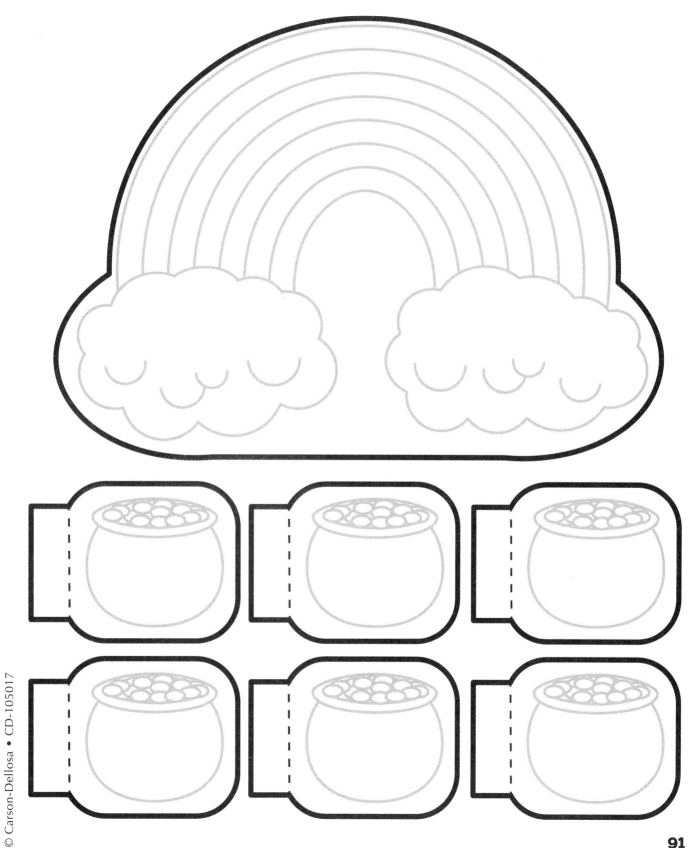

Shamrock Flaps

Cut out each shamrock flap. Apply glue to the back of the narrow section to attach it to a notebook page.

Flower Petal Fold

Cut out the flower on the solid lines. Then, fold the flaps toward the center and back out. Apply glue to the back of the center panel to attach it to a notebook page.

Kite Flap Books

Cut out the kites and bow flap books around the outside borders. Glue the kites to a notebook page and draw a kite string for each kite. Then, apply glue to the backs of the center sections to attach the bows to the notebook page below each kite. If desired, use only one kite and any number of bows.

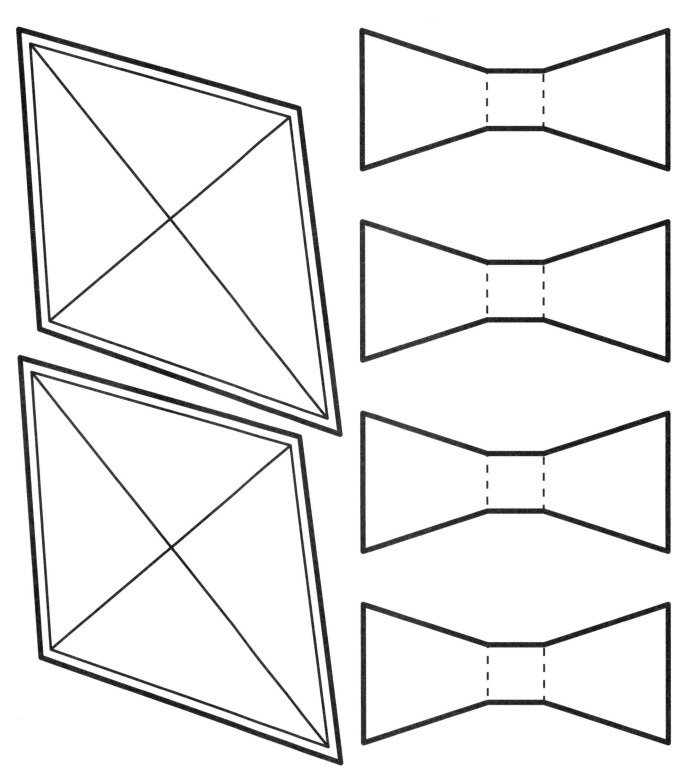

Nest Pockets with Eggs

Cut out the nest pockets on the solid lines. Apply glue to the backs of the three narrow sections on each pocket and attach one or both to a notebook page. Cut out the egg pieces and place them in the nest(s).

Twin Ice Pop Accordion Folds

Cut out the accordion pieces on the solid lines. Fold the left and right sides toward the center on the dashed lines, alternating the fold direction. The ice pops should meet in the center. Apply glue to the back of the center section to attach it to a notebook page.

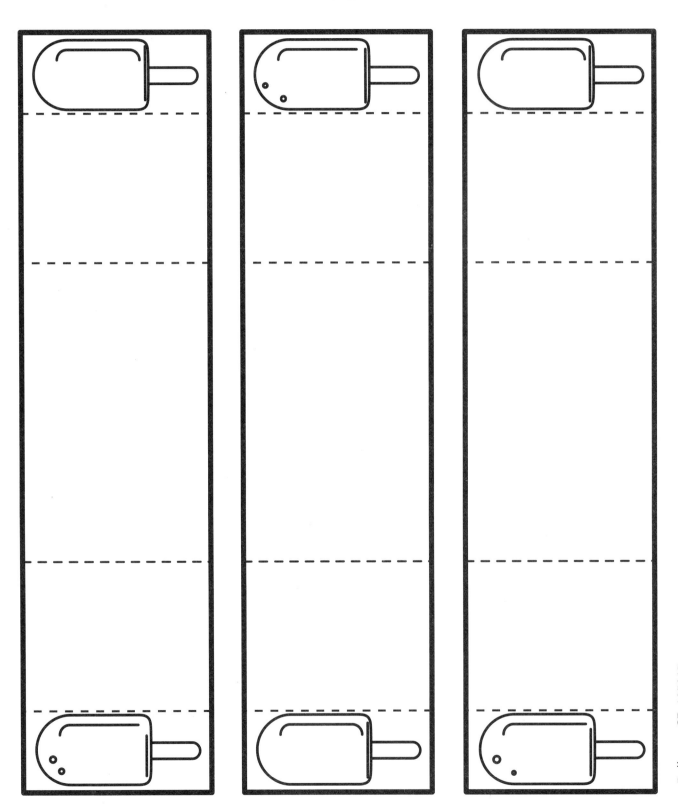